"Liz Carter offers a fresh and needed vc
pages of this book will remind you of w
one who's exhausted from striving, thes
of 'being enough,' all while growing in
sion for the least of these. A book I defi

SARAH WALTON, Author, *Hope When It Hurts*

"I've used the phrase 'used by God' many times, never stopping to interrogate
the meaning or connotations. But *Valuable* has changed that. It exposes Christian culture's misplaced obsession with usefulness. Utterly convincing in its
arguments, it presents an infinitely more wholesome vision of what God has
created us to be. As Carter puts it: 'We are recipients of God's love, and that
love comes through receiving, not through what we do'. What liberating truth!"

SAM HAILES, Editor, *Premier Christianity* **magazine**

"For those of us who grew up believing we must be better, bigger and the
best, *Valuable* is a reminder of the truth of the value we all have as God's
beloved. A gorgeous, heart-breaking, hope-bringing, astounding book. Read
it and exhale."

RACHAEL NEWHAM, Author, *Learning to Breathe* **and** *And Yet*

"Words can impact us deeply—which is why it's so important we speak wisely
and well. In this engaging book, there is encouragement to think about our
language, run back to Scripture and reassess the vocabulary of God 'using' us.
It is thought-provoking, heart-searching and conversation-starting—and a
beautiful opportunity to see more of the God who gives us value, not just use."

HELEN THORNE, Biblical Counselling UK

"The belief that we are validated through what we do is endemic in our culture
and also in the church. Many people fall off the end of that theological cliff,
exhausted, burned out or feeling like they have failed. Liz speaks a better, godly
story—of value through being, strength in weakness, extra-ordinary found in
ordinary, and a God who accepts and loves us as we are, not as we do. This
subversive, saving, Spirit-filled message is as radical as it is one of relief."

KATE MIDDLETON, Director, Mind and Soul Foundation

"If, like me, you've wanted to be useful to God, prayed that he might use
your pain, or told others they can be used by God, then read this important
book. With its clarity, beauty and fresh biblical reflection, *Valuable* is a potent
remedy to a malady we may not even realise we have—of believing ourselves
to be anything other than loved. What an important book this is."

SHERIDAN VOYSEY, Author, *The Making of Us*;
Presenter, *Pause for Thought*, **BBC Radio 2**

"Carefully applying Scripture and peppering her writing with personal illustration, Liz Carter challenges the church to reconsider its preoccupation with 'usefulness' and helps us grasp our value in the light of God's transforming love in Christ. *Valuable* is paradigm-shifting—a challenging and freeing approach to our relationship with God."

ERIC SCHUMACHER, Pastor; Author, *Worthy* **and** *Ours*

"Having benefitted hugely from Liz's writing previously, I eagerly anticipated this latest book. She writes authentically, beautifully and with great depth—as well as a thorough knowledge of Scripture. I commend this book to you—let its rich treasures of hope, truth and freedom reach deep into your soul."

CLAIRE MUSTERS, Host, Woman Alive Book Club

"A timely challenge and a profound rallying soul cry to pursue fruitfulness over usefulness. Biblical throughout, with poetic flourishes and raw, honest storytelling, Liz has done a majestic job of balancing poignant personal pain with deep teaching from the Bible. I'm so grateful to her for this message."

PHIL KNOX, Evangelical Alliance

"A brave and important book. Liz Carter invites us to explore fresh ways to approach brokenness, and to see that God's love comes through receiving, not through what we do. With its powerful and eloquent illustrations, *Valuable* is both beautiful and helpful."

WENDY VIRGO, Author, *Influential Women*

"Stripping back the notion that 'we are what we do', Liz Carter takes us on a journey of discovery, guiding us to find—or re-find—our true identity. Affirming, empathetic, encouraging and real, *Valuable* will gently reveal to you just how much you mean to God."

EMILY OWEN, Author and Speaker

"A gentle and fierce call to eschew the falsehood that our worth depends on our usefulness. Liz writes with clarity, compassion and authenticity in words that will empower everyone, from those seen as 'useful' to those who feel broken, and anywhere in between. A wonderful book."

AMY BOUCHER PYE, Author, *7 Ways to Pray* **and** *Transforming Love*

"Liz Carter beautifully challenges our values and language, which in turn challenges our culture. We all have a choice around what culture we want to build in churches, families and communities. This book, with its personal stories and theological reflections, is a gem and will be so helpful for everyone. I thoroughly recommend it."

PATRICK REGAN OBE, Co-Founder, Kintsugi Hope

LIZ CARTER

Valuable

Why your worth is
not defined by how
useful you feel

Valuable
© Liz Carter, 2023

Published by:
The Good Book Company

thegoodbook.com | thegoodbook.co.uk
thegoodbook.com.au | thegoodbook.co.nz | thegoodbook.co.in

ISBN: 9781784988661 | JOB-007280 | Printed in the UK

Design by André Parker

Contents

Foreword

Our youngest daughter, Emmaus, recently celebrated her 30th birthday. This is always a significant moment for parents, but for us it has a particular poignancy. My wife, Edrie, became seriously ill while she was carrying Emmaus and was later diagnosed with Multiple Sclerosis. So Emmaus' birthday was also the 30th anniversary of Edrie being in a wheelchair.

MS brings excruciating pain, difficulty sleeping, and a sense of helplessness—but it also brings the anguish of feeling useless. What could Edrie have achieved without this unwelcome infirmity? Couldn't we have been better parents or more productive Christians or greater prayer warriors without MS? If value is measured by productivity and success, then the things we have experienced during the last 30 years have been a massive divine mistake. We could have been so much more useful without MS.

People try to be positive. "You must be very precious to God for him to entrust you with this illness! You must be learning so many lessons!" Perhaps that is true, but did we really need to stay in the classroom that long? People want to find positive and measurable benefits of chronic illness, but sometimes there seem to be none. The same could be said of depression or broken relationships or the grief of bereavement. They leave us feeling inadequate and pathetic. We feel useless.

All of us struggle with pain of some sort or another. The only condition for suffering is to live long enough! What makes it worse is that most of us have succumbed to the lie that our value is measured by our usefulness. We start to believe that God's love is dependent on our performance. When suffering appears to limit how much God can use us, we have a problem.

In response, we might fit in place a dishonest mask—pretending that all is well, our faith is strong and the trials of this world don't touch us. Perhaps we think that if we confessed our inner struggles we would be letting the side down. Or we worry about what our brothers and sisters in church would think of us—their lives seem so together and sorted (if only we knew the truth!). So we fit our masks in place. The alternative response is to simply spiral down into despair, fearing that God has forgotten us. Edrie and I have experienced both reactions.

But in this book, with insight and sensitivity, Liz Carter maps a better route. Our value does not lie in our usefulness but in our identity as beloved children of a gracious heavenly Father.

The Puritan John Owen reminds us that God's love is "an eternal love that has no beginning and that shall have no ending; that cannot be heightened by any act of ours, that cannot be lessened by anything in us" (*Works*, 2.30). We are flawed and broken. But we are loved more than we can imagine, and God wants us to know it.

Liz reminds us that Jesus delights in small and weak things. He turns our value systems on their heads, choosing the foolish things of the world to shame the wise. Like vessels of honour in Jesus' hand, we are precious and valued. And our compassionate Saviour calls us into the fellowship of his church—the fellowship of the broken but beloved. Here we can remove our masks and find loving acceptance and transforming grace. We can experience real and liberating joy even when we cannot understand God's purpose or see the positive results of our pain.

Over the last 30 years Edrie and I have come to cherish the hope which is held out to us in the gospel. This book culminates in a celebration of the glory of that hope:

> *We've been finding ourselves in a new story of living hope, which draws us into freedom within our struggles. This hope gives us assurance that one day we will be most fully ourselves, we will be who we were created to be, we will be who we are at our very utmost.*
> *(p 117)*

Liz explores these themes and so many more in this wonderfully perceptive book.

Paul Mallard, January 2023

Introduction

"I am Nothing."

That's the despairing wail of a battered little stuffed toy in the much-loved children's book *Nothing* by Mick Inkpen. Left behind when the people in his house move away, he lies abandoned in a dusty corner of the attic. He has a feeling that once upon a time he was something, that he meant something to somebody. But now he is Nothing.

His search for who he is sends him on a painful journey where many of the voices around him only confirm his sense of insignificance. The family leaving says someone else will get rid of him. The mouse tells him the new people won't want him either. The fox says he's not even worth eating. As the little toy stares at his reflection in a pond, he sees ugliness, worthlessness and somebody who doesn't belong. He doesn't seem to have any use to anyone. "I don't know who I am," he wails.

Of course, in the end Nothing finds out that he is not Nothing at all. He was once a beloved cloth cat named Toby, and he is lovingly restored to his former glory for a new generation. He discovers that his value lies in how he is loved, no matter how he looks.

We live in a world where value and usefulness are all tangled up together. All the time, we see and hear judgments of others based on their use: "What a useless mother." "She's useless at that job." "He's a useless cook." *Shouldn't we do better? Couldn't we be better? We'd have more value if only we could be more useful.*

All of us feel a bit useless sometimes. Every day, in a thousand tiny ways, we can easily feel we are just not quite enough. Somewhere deep inside, like Nothing, we may feel like we too are on show to the critical crowds in our own lives, and we too are left staring at our reflections and found wanting.

But that is not how God sees us.

THAT LITTLE GIRL

I was the sick kid at school. The one who was always absent, always too pale and blotched with illness. As a baby I caught a serious pneumonia which started the process of scarring in my lungs that led to degenerative disease.

"You'll never amount to anything," my maths teacher told me when I was 13 years old, and I believed her. Other children only reinforced this belief in me, with their barbed words flying at me over and over again: *Useless. Hopeless. Not one of us.*

"Father, please heal Liz so she can be useful again," someone praying for me back in those days said with deep sincerity. The words reverberated in my mind and soul, casting shadows in already dark corners. It was true, after all. I *wasn't* useful. I'd never be useful; at least, not until I got healed, until I got whole.

I wondered if that was how God saw me, too. Did he see

me as no use to the kingdom, as a cast-aside, as someone who once had potential but no longer?

I can still see that little girl standing on her own in the playground if I search closely through the murk of time. She's still there somewhere, suspended and frozen, staring at her feet as the others skip away, oblivious to the power of their words. She stood still in my mind and my body for a long, long time, before I found a different script; a script which wasn't about uselessness anymore. Instead, I found a new identity as a child of God—an identity not based on what I could offer to God, but on his love for me. I finally began to fathom the depths of verses like 1 John 3 v 1:

> *See what great love the Father has lavished on us, that*
> *we should be called children of God! And that is what*
> *we are!*

And that's when I knew that I didn't have to stand on my own in the playground anymore.

A DIFFERENT SCRIPT

We form our identities around all manner of things. We grow up with people who influence us for good or bad, we go to school and hear stories about ourselves which we believe, we begin to tell ourselves our own stories, and they become part of us. Our narratives are affirmed by the world around us, by images of perfection, by others who are doing everything well. All around us we see the successful, the beautiful, the healthy, the lives which are undamaged and flawless.

The useful people.

Perhaps you feel like you could always be doing more, being more, achieving more. Maybe, like me, you live with a long-term struggle—whether in mind or body—and you can't see any way in which you can be useful to God or to others. Maybe you live with crippling grief and feel you have no way of expressing any kind of usefulness within your agony. Maybe you are neuro-diverse and feel the world often casts you aside. Maybe you feel you've messed up too many times and there's no hope for change. Maybe you've lived with a sense of uselessness for so long that it simply self-perpetuates; it loops around in your inner script and you cannot escape it.

I want to invite you on a journey beyond use and into value. It's a journey into a new framework, a better script, a freedom story. We will begin in a place of uselessness, and then go on to explore the spacious place of God's kingdom narrative, where the borders are smashed down and the script gets flipped. We'll consider the problematic language of God's use of us, and how we can apply a new language in our lives, in our weakness, in our identity and in our deepest places.

It is my prayer that as you read, you will glimpse the joyous liberation of journeying with a topsy-turvy God, who loves without conditions and slices through the lies you tell yourself. I pray that you will leave behind notions of uselessness and worthlessness as you reflect on Scripture and stories of transformation.

I pray that you will find the space beyond use, and then embrace your value in the light of a new kind of wholeness and holiness you find there.

FOR PRAYER & REFLECTION

I'm useless, I say,
I am Nothing.
My soul churns the words and
They spatter through my mind,
Daubed by a hundred ruinous brushes
Painting society's whispers and my own failures
Across the landscape of my life.
But I take a step forward,
Dare to trust a new journey
Where hope writes the lyrics and
Peace plays the melody.
Where I run into a new story
Of freedom and triumph.
Where use gets blotted out by perfect love
And I dance through golden avenues
Of upside-down glory.

1. We Are the Useless

The day was freezing, my brain was foggy and the children were small bundles of energy. I had another chest infection, fighting breathlessness, and the five-minute school run seemed like climbing a mountain in driving snow. I went to bed, spent. Then, at lunchtime, I got the call, the voice dripping with disdain: "You've forgotten your children's lunches, Mrs Carter." And there it was. The *Useless* word hit me, screaming through my mind, reminding me of all the past uselessnesses, large and small. I was a useless mother who couldn't even manage to feed her children.

We speak uselessness over ourselves for many reasons. Some of us are sad. Some of us are sick. Some of us are just weary. Some of us have failed; some of us think we have failed even when we haven't. Some of us look at the lives of others and think that we are useless in comparison.

Perhaps you picked up this book because you feel like you are useless. Maybe you believe that if you were just a little bit more useful, you would be worth more. Perhaps you look in the mirror and you say, *Useless*. You burn a cake and you say, *Useless*. You mess up something at work and you say, *Useless*. You shout at your child and you say, *Useless*.

This sense of uselessness can spill over into our faith, too. How we see ourselves influences how we think God sees us, and how we feel about ourselves in our church communities. In church and in groups, we might feel like we're always saying the wrong thing, or we just don't know enough. We feel as though we can't be useful because we're not very good at reading the Bible, or praying, or spending time in worship. Maybe we don't feel we're enough because everyone else seems to have a lovely home to welcome others into, and we live in a shabby flat.

It would be great to be properly used by God, we might think—to be part of God's plan for reaching others and making a difference. But how can we be, when we feel so useless?

THE DREGS OF SOCIETY
When I was 13 years old, my family went to live with the forgotten people.

My dad became the vicar of a struggling church on a poverty-stricken estate in Birmingham in central England. The congregation were terrified of the local community, where crime levels were high. A young girl had been raped in the church grounds not long before we arrived. A renowned local gang used our front garden and walls as their meeting place, taking drugs, having sex in plain sight and threatening my family. We were uprooted and lost, shipwrecked and bewildered, unable to understand why God had called us to such a hideous place.

All around us, local people were known as the underclass, the dregs of society, the scum. They descended from generations of people who thought themselves nothing; people who'd lived in the inner-city slums and were then rehoused in the post-war clearances. The new estates were supposed to bring hope, but instead became places of fear. Unemployment was high and there was an assumption that these people were unemployable. They themselves lived deep inside these assumptions—it was hard-wired in them that they were without use, so they might as well forget trying to get a job. They were thought of as useless, and they thought of themselves as useless, too, disempowered to combat the story told about them for so long. Outside the estates the middle-class suburbs looked on with distaste and distrust; here were the undeserving, the unproductive, the useless. *Stay away from them.*

ANGELS ON THE WALLS
The gang that made our front lawn, our walls and the front of the church their headquarters were greatly feared locally and avoided at all costs—but we couldn't avoid them. Every day we ran the gauntlet through the jeers and the cursing, the thrown bottles and bricks, and the explicit threats, and I would go to school in tears, my world falling apart. My mother was stretched to breaking point, and began to stay up at night screaming at God: "Why have you brought us here? Why have you taken us out of a safe place into this? Why have you abandoned us?" My parents longed to build a church with and for these people, to serve them and welcome them into our family, to rewrite the useless script that so many held. But at this point it was difficult to see

how we could even begin. We felt under siege in a strange land. (You can read more of this story in the book *Angels on the Walls* by Wallace and Mary Brown.)

One night, after months of this torture, Mum sensed God leading her to the book of Nehemiah, where she discovered a story about walls under siege. After the people of Israel came back from exile in Babylon, the city of Jerusalem lay in ruins and Nehemiah was charged to lead the rebuilding project. However, they were opposed by the governor of Samaria, who stirred up a rebellion against the rebuilders. Nehemiah's response was prayer and action:

But we prayed to our God and posted a guard day and night to meet this threat. (Nehemiah 4 v 9)

I remember so clearly the next morning, when Mum came into the kitchen bright-eyed and enthusiastic, brandishing her Bible at my dad. "It's all here in Nehemiah," she said. "This is what God's telling us to do. Pray and put guards on the walls."

Dad looked unconvinced. Like we could afford to employ security guards 24/7…

Mum quickly became frustrated. "Not actual guards. Don't be silly. God means that we should pray and station *angels* on the walls."

"Of course," Dad said, rolling his eyes. But Mum always won the arguments in our house. All of us were marshalled, me and my brothers and a small, bemused group of church people, and we walked around the garden and grounds of the church, stopping by the walls and praying that God would place his angels there. We felt rather silly, really—

which was compounded by the mockery from gang members who sprawled over the lawn.

The next day, only about half the gang members turned up.

The day after that, only about five.

The day after that, none.

They never came back. People asked if they'd just gone elsewhere to terrorise others, but we found out later (from a gang member who had become a Christian) that they just didn't want to do it anymore. God had worked in their hearts to bring this violence and hatred to a halt. From then on, people streamed into the church, drawn by something they couldn't quite understand.

God sometimes answers prayer in the most unexpected and miraculous ways. But the main reason I tell this story is to demonstrate how God feels about so-called "useless" people. With this miracle, God began a work in this ragged, broken community, redirecting their plot, reversing this ingrained story written upon them for many generations. As time went on, we had the privilege of witnessing the impact of the power and liberty of the gospel on many of these crushed lives. Here is the first thing I want to make clear: every single person is valuable to God. We are all bearers of his image (Genesis 1 v 27-28) and he knows each hair of our head (Luke 12 v 7). God loves us with a love far greater than we can imagine, no matter how useless we feel, no matter how much our own stories have become cages of worthlessness.

But that's not all…

THE PRODUCTIVITY LIE

What do you do? Most people think that this is just an innocent, getting-to-know-you question. But a darkness lies beneath. Because this is often the first question folk ask, our work seems like it must be the most important thing about us. The question implies that we are validated through what we do.

I remember moving to a new town, having left my work as a primary school teacher due to further lung damage from a complex pneumonia. The first time I was asked, "What do you do?" I was caught short: what *do* I do? I fumbled through an answer—I was looking for a new job, I'd been ill, I was a teacher between jobs. I justified myself through my status as a professional-who'd-be-back-in-work-soon, but it seemed hollow. I soon felt I had nothing to offer if I could not be defined by my career.

There's a productivity lie entrenched in our society. Wherever we look, we see signs of it. Adverts draw us towards a link between our productivity and success, and the acquisition of material goods. Social media lauds the useful people, those who achieve. People post photos of their children's school successes, but tend to keep the failures hidden. In the UK, the welfare reforms of the 2010s sparked a narrative that said there were those who tried hard and those who shirked—"the strivers and the skivers". Those who contributed to society were more deserving of help than those who didn't. And many of the most vulnerable were left in an even weaker position.

We so often tie our identity to our achievements, because that's what the world shouts from every corner. Even in times of rest or exhaustion we hear that nagging voice whispering: *You should be doing more. You should finish that project. You should be better at that.*

I had to "shield" through much of 2020 and 2021 because

I was pronounced clinically extremely vulnerable to Covid. Some of the discussion around the pandemic floored me and dragged me down into a further sense of uselessness. It was as though there was a new shift in the way people talked about "the vulnerable".

Covid was mainly hitting those with underlying conditions: the old and the sick. The country seemed to be presented with a choice: save the vulnerable, or save the economy? A large section of society saw it as unfair that their lives were on pause because of people who were, as they put it, just going to die anyway. Meanwhile, economic considerations—the productivity of the country—were claimed by some to be more important than containing Covid. Why should we shut up the shops and stop workers from working, just to give the vulnerable a few more years? The debate was complex, of course, with lockdowns and restrictions causing untold harm as well, but still those of us categorised as clinically vulnerable experienced words like these as punches to our guts: it was as though we mattered less than the healthy. Usefulness mattered more.

This is the productivity lie. And it has no place in our faith.

THE MANY CAGES OF USELESSNESS

Uselessness can be a script in our minds. We don't have to live in great sickness or poverty to feel useless, because the word is written over us in many ways, every day, as we browse the internet, comparing, comparing, comparing. Uselessness is endemic in a society that elevates the strong and the beautiful. It weaves its way through our minds and hisses insidious whispers at us: *we ought to be better.*

Some of us experience the depths of uselessness, and some of us the very edges of it, but whatever level it strikes us at, it harms our view of self and our view of how God sees us. We're not just useless, we think—we're useless *to God*. And that's a deeper hurt.

Maybe you recognise some words and phrases like these ones. Maybe these have been applied to your life, by you or by others:

- I am rubbish at anything academic. I never did well at school, so there's no point me thinking I could achieve anything now.
- I am plain and ugly. Even my parents said I would never turn heads.
- I'm a bit useless in social situations. In my church small group I just sit there in silence. I can't seem to find words.
- I don't have any talents or gifts. I hear people saying everyone has a talent, a gift from God, but I'm not good at anything.
- I'm not good enough as a parent. I keep letting my children down. I don't know the right way to teach them about God.
- I can't shake off this grief. I'll never be any use to anyone.
- I've hurt pretty much everyone I love. There's no help for someone like me.
- I'm too sick to be of any use to the world, or to God. I can't even make it to church regularly.
- I feel overwhelmed by life. Christians are supposed to be committed and servant-hearted, but I have little energy. I'm always cancelling on people.

- People think I am coping, but they don't see what
lies beneath. The more they praise me, the more of
a fraud I feel.

I'm sure you could add your own inner narrative to this
list. Maybe there's even something you haven't consciously
understood, but you sense it there, clawing away at you. If
only you could be more useful, more worthy, you think.

RAHAB THE USEFUL?

I've often heard our sense of being useless challenged in
this way: we *can* be useful to God—just look at Moses, for
example! He was so weak, and look how God used him!
When we dig into Scripture, we do indeed find a whole
lot of people who we might see as being used by God and
useful to his purposes. We might even say that because
these people were useful, we can be too.

This sounds positive, doesn't it? Uselessness can be transformed to usefulness. But it leaves a hollowed-out understanding of the truth of what God was doing in these stories
and still does in our lives.

Let's reflect for a moment on the story of Rahab in
Joshua 2.

Rahab was amongst the lowest of the low. She was a hated
Canaanite, and even among her own countrymen she was
despised because of her trade. A harlot, they called her, a
woman of the night. A whore. She had no use in society
apart from the use of her body by others.

Two Israelites turned up at her door, spies sent by Joshua,
seeking safe haven. She knew Canaanites were hated and
feared by Israelites, yet she took them into her home. It's
likely they found her door because she lived in a strategic

position in the city walls, and because it wasn't unusual to see unknown men go in and out of her house. But something was different about these two, and something wonderful happened to Rahab as she sheltered them: she was filled with the knowledge of who their God was.

The LORD your God is God in heaven above and on the earth below. (Joshua 2 v 11)

She had heard the stories of Israel, the great stories of how God had parted the Red Sea and overcome their enemies, and in this moment she believed. And because she believed, she risked her life to protect these spies from the king of Jericho.

Rahab was useful to God; yes, we could say that. We might even say that God used her. She sheltered the spies and ultimately Jericho fell. A useless woman became useful.

But that's not the heart of what happened, is it?

I believe that we are mistaken when we view these stories merely through the lens of *use*. God countered the story written over Rahab's life: in God's narrative she was not Rahab the fallen woman, Rahab the reviled, but Rahab the restored. Whoever she had been before the arrival of the spies from Israel, God transformed her; she became a new creation. Would it be just, then, to say that Rahab was merely useful to God and God's purposes? Wasn't there something deeper at play, something about a woman who had experienced a harsh life, filled with abuse and hate, being transformed by a God who had more in mind than her usefulness?

It seems to me that God's priorities here are obvious in the details. Her desperate, harsh life; her profession of belief; her willingness to risk her life; and the way her scarlet cord features in the story. Scarlet was a symbol of who she had been and the life she had been steeped in, a symbol of pain and bloodshed and hatred—a scarlet cord for a scarlet woman—and this was the item God chose to use. In fact, God flipped the meaning of the cord from an object of shame to a symbol of hope and commitment to God's purposes.

God didn't *use* Rahab. He loved her. He transformed her.

Rahab, the lowest of the low, became the mother of a man named Boaz, a man who would go on to turn society's view of the weak and the useless on its head in his honour of Ruth when she was destitute and helpless, loving her with the redeeming and generous love of God. He echoed the love of his mother, the love God showered upon her in her own weakness and status as the hated. Rahab's actions streamed through history, her perceived uselessness transformed into great acclaim as she took her place as great-great-grandmother of King David, and ancestor of Jesus Christ.

This is so characteristic of our God, who loves to turn the story around, who loves to take the scorned things and turn them into honour. Rahab's life was arrested in darkness and turned into beauty. She became one of the most revered women in Scripture, included in a handful of women mentioned in the genealogy of Jesus in Matthew 1. Rahab discovered the saving power of God that blazed into her darkness and set her and her family free. Let's honour her, then, along with Scripture, remembering her remarkable story—a story which encapsulates so much more than just usefulness. Let's honour her by understanding our own stories the same way we understand hers.

TRANSFORMING THE STORY

Uselessness is a cage, but it can be a blanket as well. Sometimes we shroud ourselves in it, a familiar, tatty old thing from childhood, something we think represents who we really are. It can even feel like a relief to draw the blanket around ourselves. At least we know where we are with it, after all.

Unfortunately, the more we huddle under the blanket, the more the old story will become our present story, as we allow the words to take root in our souls.

What about you? Do you see a sense of uselessness as a cage around you—something imposed upon you, something you cannot break free from—or as more of a security blanket, something you've lived with so long you don't want to throw it away, however dirty and scrappy it is?

In this book we are going to turn the tide and explore the not-good-enough language we have so often taken on. We're going to celebrate God's work in people who feel like they have no use or no worth, and we're going to find out that we have far more worth than we could imagine. We're going to plunge into places of transformation, where we find golden invitations into a deeper understanding of who we are in God.

But there's something more, too. In this book we are going to flip the narrative. I want to tackle the productivity lie and show that it's possible—and that it's biblical—to throw out the narrative of use entirely. What if you could not only reject the label *useless* but completely reframe that language? What if you could think of yourself the way you think of Rahab?

How can we begin to change the script? In the next

chapter we will start to think about what our new frame-work could be—and it's something with enough power to trample old words and spark new wonder.

FOR PRAYER & REFLECTION

*Father, when I am weighed under a burden of
uselessness,
Chase away the words that wound
And whisper your words of love.
When I am trod under the foot of a world that discounts me,
Remind me of my worth in you
And whisper your words of truth.
When I speak uselessness over myself,
Shatter apart my empty words
And whisper your words of hope.
Amen.*

- Think about the story you find yourself in. Have the words and actions of others caged you into a script of uselessness? Have your own self-accusations bound you even tighter?

- How did Rahab's story make you feel? Reflect on the way God transformed her story from a tale of uselessness to a chronicle of honour and joy. Was Rahab merely useful to God?

2. Into the Upside Down

He is desperate.

Nineteen years a slave, shackled into a chain gang, left with nothing to make his way in the world. Given shelter by a bishop, he is bewildered by the unexpected generosity but still feels chained in; there's no hope, no choice but to steal the bishop's silver. He has to eat, after all. He has to survive.

Jean knows that if he is caught, he will be arrested. Probably executed, given his history, and knowing the power structures of the society he lives in. When he is seized by police, he is resigned to the consequences.

Then his world is tipped upside down. The bishop makes a wild claim to the police: Jean didn't steal those items, he says, because he, the bishop, gave them to him as a gift. As he places them back in Jean's hands, Jean knows he is looking into the face of abundant, outrageous grace, instead of condemnation. From that time on, his life and his journey are transformed.

This story from Victor Hugo's *Les Misérables* gives us a glimpse into something profound about the true story of God: it gives us a picture of a countercultural kingdom, where norms and expectations are reversed, and the useless are honoured.

It gives us a window into the Upside Down.

REVERSE DIRECTION

In the card game *Uno*, various cards give instructions about how the game should proceed. When my children were young, they were especially keen on the cards that change the outcome of the game for someone else: pick up four, miss a turn, change colour. But the card that most often changes the course of the game is the "reverse direction" card, where the players must change the direction of play. The player who was about to win is left frustrated as someone else takes her place. The last becomes first in one swift move.

We've seen how uselessness and use in general can form a framework for the way in which we see ourselves and interact with God. To break free from this oppressive framework, we need to play the reverse direction card. We need to turn the game around so that we can put fears into perspective; we need to twist our scripts of uselessness until the words tumble out and disappear from the page. Let's zoom out and catch hold of the bigger picture of how God responds to those who are weak and worn out. In the next chapter, we will zero in on the language of use—what do we really mean when we say God uses people? First of all, though, we're going to look wider. We're going to plunge into God's countercultural kingdom, and explore our place within it. We're going to immerse ourselves in the Upside Down. This is where wrongs are righted, where value is proclaimed, and where grace and truth mix together to form a new story of justice, mercy, peace and everlasting life.

A LIBRARY FULL OF USELESSNESS
Jesus likes the small and weak things.

Take a tiny sparrow. Why would Jesus pick this bird for an illustration when he has his whole creation full of avian wonder at his disposal? Surely he would choose something beautiful, something blazing with glory and colour. Maybe he would pick something with great strength and majesty, like an eagle, or something fast and dazzling, like a falcon. Perhaps a wise owl, or a graceful heron. But instead Jesus spotlights the most common of birds: a bird with a simple chirrup that can barely be called a song.

Jesus chooses an example of weakness to paint a picture about how precious each one of us is. Even a common bird like a sparrow does not escape his Father's notice, he says, and if God cares for each tiny sparrow, how much more does God care for us? In fact, we are more valuable than many sparrows (Matthew 10 v 29-31). To Jesus' first-century audience, the idea of every person, including the weakest, being of so much worth to God would be radical—even dangerous.

But Jesus uses an ordinary bird to make an extraordinary point.

Jesus does this again and again in his parables and his interactions with people. He doesn't use the examples that his culture would expect or see as worthy of honour. Instead, he chooses the weak, the weary and the foolish. He chooses the tax collectors and sends the rich away empty-handed. He spins tales of banquets where the poor and disabled are welcome and honoured.

Through the sweeping history of the Bible, we see this kind of reverse-direction story played out often in the people God chooses to partner with. In fact, we could call the Bible a library full of uselessness. From the start we see people who mess up, with Adam and Eve deceiving, Abraham doubting and attempting to twist God's hand, Sarah lying, Joseph bragging—and ending up dumped in a pit for his efforts. We have Moses, all prepared to quit because he's not a natural speaker; Aaron, who speaks for him but then crafts other gods; the Israelites whinging about how much they miss cucumbers. We see Gideon, weakest of his clan, and Elijah, who wishes to die, weary and depressed. We journey with Ruth and Naomi, empty and without hope in a world where women are destitute without men; and then we read of David, the youngest (but God looks at the heart, of course). We witness Jeremiah trying to deny his call, believing he's too young, and Jonah running from God.

We travel alongside Mary, young and unmarried, and sceptical Nathanael, and James and John, who beg for a higher status. We cringe with Peter, betraying Jesus in his darkest hour, and empathise with doubting Thomas. We sense the pain of the thorn slicing Paul's side. And above all, we see Jesus, dying in agony, the starkest example of God's power being played out in great weakness.

Many of these people might be seen as failures, even useless, in their culture and in ours. But all of them took their place in a greater story, where God worked with them and through them. Some might say that they were all used by God and useful to God's purposes, but I believe that their stories warrant a far greater triumph and dignity. They weren't merely useful to God—the truth is, he turned their lives inside out.

THE UPSIDE-DOWN CHOCOLATE FACTORY

It was the late 19th century, and Jemima Ayres' husband Charles had just died. He was too young.

Jemima was terrified of the future, bringing up four daughters alone on a rural farm with little income. How would they survive? One day, in Birmingham, delivering some of their farm produce, she noticed a battered greengrocer's shop for sale on the Pershore Road, at a price she could just about afford. She moved there with her daughters, but soon realised that the shop income wasn't covering her overheads. She needed her daughters to find work. But she was worried about them—would they find work in a safe place? Would they be exploited, as young and pretty girls so often were in the city?

As she settled into the area, Jemima began to hear good things about the new chocolate factory not far away. She heard about how they looked after their workers, and about the beautiful grounds and recreational facilities. Few businesses offered an ethos like this in the Victorian era, where work was harsh and workers were utilities. Jemima wanted this life for her girls—but would a big firm like Cadbury's take on young girls who had fallen on hard times?

From the birth of the business in a tiny shop in the early 19th century, the Cadbury family had established a culture of unlikely grace in the dark age of the Industrial Revolution. Most similar companies kept their workers in grinding poverty, with poor housing and desperate living and working conditions, but the Cadbury family held a fundamentally different outlook. In 1878, George Cadbury had a vision for a better life for their workers: "Why should an industrial area be squalid and depressing?" he asked. They moved the factory to a new premises in what is now Bournville ("a factory in a garden"), and they built houses around the factory. Instead of replicating the dark and squalid "tunnel-back" houses of workers in industrial Birmingham, they built light and airy houses on wide tree-lined roads, with good sanitation and gardens with vegetable patches. (You can read more about all of this at www.cadbury.co.uk/about-bournville.)

The Cadbury family's devout Christian faith underpinned their vision for their workers. As Quakers in those times, they were radical followers of Jesus and his teachings. They saw their work as an opportunity to play out God's principles of justice, righteousness, and mercy.

Every morning they held prayers for all the staff. They didn't see their employees as worker bees, but as human beings, worthy of respect; they provided sick pay, education, retirement income and opportunities to improve health. They employed many more women than the average, awarding them competitive wages. As well as providing all these things for their workers, the Cadbury brothers fought for reform and freedom from oppression for people who lived in the inner-city slums.

Jemima Ayres was my great-great-grandmother. She was drawn by the ethos of the company, and even more so when three of her daughters were taken on (the fourth, Ada, my great-grandmother, helped in the shop). The girls thrived, given opportunities they would never have dreamed of. In a world where women needed a man to survive, Jemima's tenacity and the Cadburys' crazy generosity reversed the direction for this family.

The Cadbury story is one soaked in kindness, justice, and revolutionary social action. They believed the bigger God-story and put it into action, even though all around them they saw business models that valued profits over people. It is my story, too. My grandmother met my grandfather when they were both employed by Cadbury's, young people without qualifications given opportunities they were bowled over by.

When Jemima built a house at the back of her shop in 1900 with the help of her daughters' earnings, she called it Hope House. I am so grateful for an upside-down factory that weaved an aroma of (chocolatey) grace through the lives of so many. I am grateful that this grace gave my great-great-grandmother hope and a future.

As with the upside-down stories we find in Scripture, we see in this story God's kingdom in action. We see a chocolate company drawing its employees out of desperation and into a new, unexpected hope—because God's inside-out kingdom did not stop with the Bible. In following Jesus and prioritising the weak, the Cadbury family give us a beautiful example of what it is to bring a grace-filled culture to the factory floor.

Honour for those who are weaker lies at the heart of the gospel. Pity, and even kindness, are not enough—it's when we adopt a whole new way of life, one that centres on kingdom principles, that we see transformation in ourselves and in our communities. Right from the start of his ministry, Jesus declared this holy manifesto: *Blessed are the poor, the hungry, those who weep* (Luke 6 v 20-21). He'd been sent to proclaim release to the captives, to bring good news to the poor (Luke 4 v 18-19). He spoke of the kingdom God had prepared from the foundation of the world as a place where the hungry are fed, the thirsty given water, the stranger welcomed, the naked clothed, the sick cared for and the prisoners visited (Matthew 25 v 34-36).

Of course, to many in his audience, the idea of this kind of kingdom would have been sheer foolishness.

SWITCHING POWER COMPANIES

I gazed around the cathedral, in awe of its beauty and craftsmanship, the lofty arches and hushed footsteps. Hundreds of years of worship seemed to echo through the sanctuary. Then, all at once, the cathedral lost its lustre for me. I saw the tombs at the front, in pride of place: city councilmen, mayors, dukes. All the important people, the men who'd held power in that city. These were the people remembered and honoured in this holy place. What a wrongful reversal of Jesus' commands! I was reminded of something I'd read about a particular church in the US where the first two rows were reserved for VIPs and celebrities.

Power was a big deal to people who lived in 1st-century Corinth, too. A Greek city rebuilt by Julius Caesar, it was a central hub of Greco-Roman culture, architecture and intellectualism. Renowned scholars and philosophers would stand in the marketplace sharing their thoughts with huge audiences who came from far and wide to hear their wisdom. Factions were built up, arguing among themselves about who the best teachers were.

Some of the Christians in Corinth began to fall into this way of thinking. They were taking sides when it came to the apostles—some followed Paul, some Apollos, some Peter (1 Corinthians 1 v 12). Paul stopped them in their tracks, urging a better way. He drew a line of stark contrast between the power they were used to and the wisdom and power of the gospel.

> *Jews demand signs and Greeks look for wisdom, but we preach Christ crucified: a stumbling-block to Jews and foolishness to Gentiles, but to those whom God has called, both Jews and Greeks, Christ the power of God and the wisdom of God. For the foolishness of God is wiser than human wisdom, and the weakness of God is stronger than human strength.*
> *(1 Corinthians 1 v 22-25)*

For the Jews, the message of the gospel was one huge obstacle. The idea of a crucified Messiah would have been scandalous to them; the cross was the worst, most shameful death possible if you followed the Law of Moses. The historian Tom Holland says that the Jewish-Roman world would have found the idea of a crucified Messiah "beyond weird" and an "outrage" ("How St Paul Changed the World", *Unbelievable* podcast, 20th July 2018). They would never have interpreted Isaiah 53, which predicts the death of Jesus, as a messianic prophecy; the idea of the Messiah as "despised and rejected" and "pierced for our transgressions" would have appalled Jews, who were expecting a political Messiah, a hero to deliver them from the oppression of the Romans. How could the Messiah be someone so powerless, when they were completely hemmed in by power that controlled and trampled them?

For Gentiles, living in a Roman colony, the gospel message would have been laughable idiocy. Power was their foundation, and they'd come to revere the highbrow rationalism of their celebrity teachers. Who was this guy, who couldn't even speak with eloquence (v 17), saying all these things about a crucified Saviour from a race of people they hated? It was preposterous.

It wasn't only that the gospel made no sense to them. It was the fact that Jesus was flipping the power structure. As Tom Holland tells us, Roman power was "affirmed by brutality". Men in positions of power had the right to torture, burn and murder anyone they wished to. But Paul was presenting a defiantly subversive challenge: power came in weakness and foolishness. Jesus, dying on the cross, became the most dynamic example of true power possible. His death atoned for every human sin, giving us access to God and drawing us into peace and hope (Romans 5 v 1-2). His resurrection demonstrated God's ultimate victory over death, filling us with the same power, born in weakness (Ephesians 1 v 19-20). All the power of the world is powerless beside it.

OUR WISE AND STRONG THINGS

We, too, live in a world that scorns the gospel and elevates the powerful. Paul's words are as potent now as they were for the first Christians. They remind us that God came to upend power and honour weakness.

But God chose the foolish things of the world to shame the wise; God chose the weak things of the world to

> *shame the strong. God chose the lowly things of this*
> *world and the despised things—and the things that*
> *are not—to nullify the things that are, so that no one*
> *may boast before him. (1 Corinthians 1 v 27-29)*

What are the things we boast in? Who are the strong people? Who are the intellectuals we follow and laud? The answers play out across the canvas of social media. When we scroll through our feeds, we see worldly power in action. We may not be governed by violent cultists who can suppress and murder us, but we are governed by the way others on these platforms make us feel. We see the beautiful, talented people, the perfect families, the children who achieve, the Christians who have their lives sorted. We see celebrities with flawless bodies and people of much higher intelligence than us.

And we keep hearing the same words: *God uses these kinds of people so powerfully.* Our power feels drained in comparison, and we curl back into uselessness.

But Paul's radical message utterly upends this narrative: "no one may boast", he writes. Worldly power, riches and acclaim are not the power base of God's topsy-turvy kingdom.

Jesus didn't overthrow the Romans, but he overthrew the very basis of power itself. He overthrew earthly power through his revolutionary teachings, with talk of turning the other cheek and of fathers who forgive, of justice for the poor and inclusion for those who were hated; with words of scorn for the powerful and rebuke for the hypocrites, and words of love for the lost. He overthrew power by laying aside his rights as the Son of God, and, most of all, by suffering and dying.

He toppled the power of this world by making a kingdom of strength into a kingdom of foolishness. And we have this insurgent, incendiary, upside-down framework of radical reversals upon which to build our identities and throw out uselessness.

If you're feeling useless, weak, crushed or foolish, this kingdom is for you.

WELCOME TO THE UPSIDE DOWN

Welcome to a new story with a new kind of kingdom. Welcome to a love without borders and without a whole world's worth of unhelpful social mores.

Welcome to the Upside Down.

As we go forward to explore new ways to reframe the limiting language of use, let's think for a moment about one particular encounter with Jesus, and take it along with us on the journey. It's an encounter that brought freedom and dignity to a person who was seen as the most useless in her society.

Mark 5 v 21-34 tells the story of the woman with an issue of bleeding who came to Jesus and received miraculous healing. She was used to being the isolated one, the untouchable. She'd been bleeding for twelve years. *Unclean*, the daily whispers sounded around her. She'd heard about this man of healing, and the stories ignited a spark within her. What if she just touched the edge of his cloak?

He knew someone had touched him—he'd felt the power leave him. It was an acute situation; desperation hung in the air. And Jesus stopped. Jesus took time to search this woman out, to honour her faith, to speak peace and hope over her and call her by a tender name.

But Jesus kept looking around to see who had done it
... He said to her, "Daughter, your faith has healed
you. Go in peace and be freed from your suffering."
(Mark 5 v 32-34)

In speaking to this woman, Jesus was undermining prevailing power structures and communicating God's value for every human being—man or woman, sick or healthy. The Pharisees in the crowd would have been outraged at his response: associating with a woman, a banished woman at that? Others would have been frustrated: Jesus was supposed to be on the way to see a dying child. Why was he lingering?

But Jesus wasn't just making a point about the reversal of power. He was flooding an individual—an individual seen as useless and worthless—with divine love.

He was reversing the narrative of her life.

And he is searching the crowd for you, too, calling you forward, welcoming you into his surprising, glorious Upside Down. Are you ready to step towards him?

Are you ready to touch his cloak?

FOR PRAYER & REFLECTION

Jesus, when I am bowed down
Under the weight of power that crushes,
Remind me of your inside-out power.
Saturate me in the foolish things, the weak things,
The truth of dynamic grace in desperate suffering.
Immerse me in your Upside Down,
Assure me of my worth in you
Even when I feel of no use in the sight of others.
Transform my story, O Lord,
As I pin my eyes on you
And hear you call me with words of tenderness.
Amen.

- Reflect on the story of the woman with bleeding. Read the passage slowly, and then read it again, immersing yourself in the sounds and the sights, the heaving of the crowd, the desperation of Jairus. Listen to Jesus' voice as he speaks to the woman. How will you allow him to change your story, today?

- What are the power structures in your life? Think about what you spend your time on and what feeds you: social media, the acclaim of others, TV shows. How could the passage from 1 Corinthians help you break free?

3. God Is Not
a User

A few years ago, an image was shared far and wide among Christians on the internet, with these words superimposed: "God is looking for people to use, and if you can get usable, he will wear you out. The most dangerous prayer you can pray is this: 'Use me'."

Use. Usable. Use Me.

Words like these have landed on me in some of my darkest moments, when I've felt as though others all around me are being used by God, and I am not, because I am too weak. I am already too worn out. I hear all the great stories of those who are used most, and they are supposed to inspire me, but they repress me. I read quotes like this and they are supposed to envision me, but they subdue me.

These words are not meant to be oppressive. We mean them for good. But they can strike at the heart in times of fragility and exhaustion—times when life's push towards usefulness feels most unrelenting.

THE DISCORDANT CHIMES OF GOD THE USER

God can use you. That's what they say. You believe it… you think. But perhaps there's something more going on here, something you react to at a visceral level, something *wrong*. You're just not sure what it is.

Perhaps we can break it down like this: what is your initial response to these titles—taken from real blog posts and books?

- Can God use you after divorce?
- God can use you in spite of your weakness
- God uses broken people for his glory
- Hey God, I'm a woman! Can you use me?
- Got a weakness? God can use you!
- God uses the timid, the imperfect and the underdogs
- 50 ways to be used by God

What's wrong with these? God *can* use us, right? God can use anybody! It's what everyone has always said, after all.

But is it what the Bible says?

In this chapter we're going to explore the word "use" in Scripture, especially in the context of the imagery of "vessels" and "pots"—useful things, yet items from which Paul draws vibrant analogies to draw us deeper into passionate faith. We're going to think about what it really means to relate to God as the potter, and what that means in terms of "God uses" language.

This is important because words matter. Words have the power to build up and break down. Words can sink deep into our minds and our spirits, and sometimes we don't even realise the damage they are doing.

Consider this scenario:

She'd been used all her life. First by her parents, who'd seen her as some kind of unpaid servant. Then by friends. Then by the men. One after the other, they had told her they loved her, but it was all a lie. Each one of them had used her: for sex, for her money, to boost their own image. They had used her and then they had discarded her.

Used. Used. Used all the way through life.

Then her new Christian friend told her that God could use her…

We don't tend to stop to think about this kind of language, because it's so familiar. We don't hear the word "use" or its meaning as unhelpful, let alone destructive, in this context. We hear the encouragement—God wants to work in all our lives, whatever we have done and however weak we are.

But if we stop for a moment and think about this kind of well-intentioned phrasing, we might soon be taken aback.

GOD CAN ~~EXPLOIT~~ ~~MANIPULATE~~ USE YOU

You might think this is a somewhat inflammatory subtitle. After all, when we talk about God using people, we don't have anything like this in mind at all.

Yet normally when we talk about somebody using another person, the phrase does not carry positive connotations—as in the above scenario. "Used" would usually refer to a person used for money, sex or power, then discarded.

We might think of "God using" language as helpful and even comforting, but how do others hear it and experience it? What if to the world around us it is dissonant and strange—and maybe even worse? What if it carries heavy overtones of toxic power and control?

Have a look at some of the synonyms for "use" listed in thesaurus.com:

> *USE: Control, exploit, handle, manage, manipulate,*
> *spend, utilise, wield, capitalise, exhaust, expend,*
> *govern, waste, press into service, take advantage of.*

Do these words represent God's work in our lives? Can you imagine trying to comfort someone struggling with worthlessness with the words "You don't need to feel lesser, because God can control you"? When you are weary and weak, how would you feel if a friend said, "You're so much more than you think. God can exploit you!"

You'd be outraged, of course, and probably deeply hurt. This kind of language would have the effect of turning you against God—and against the friend who used the words.

I don't believe we are consciously inferring these kinds of implications when we do say the words "God can use you". But what if these words feed into something at a more subliminal level? What if we experience these words as a condemnation, unable to see how we can possibly be "used" in our situation? What if we are hearing echoes of some of these destructive synonyms because of past experience of being used by others?

Generally, this language is meant for blessing and enrichment. Christians have developed it to "encourage one another and build each other up" (1 Thessalonians 5 v 11). But given the connotations around this language in our world, perhaps it is time to review the way we speak, in order to live in obedience to this verse in a much more extensive and generous way.

DOES GOD USE PEOPLE IN THE BIBLE?

The interesting thing about phrases like these, so well used within Christianity, is that there is an underlying assumption that they are biblical. When we say "God can use you", we think we are quoting Scripture, or at least the spirit of Scripture. We think about all those Bible characters who were used by God, and we surmise that the words themselves must regularly feature in the text. There are a few other phrases like this, so well worn that they are seen as biblical: "God helps those who help themselves", "Money is the root of all evil", "God works in mysterious ways", "God won't give you more than you can handle", "Cleanliness is next to godliness". None of these quotes are in the Bible—in fact, some of them directly oppose the message of the gospel.

The same is true of "God can use you". In the Old Testament, the word "use" itself only appears in 62 verses (NIV) and never in the context we are exploring. (Tim Carter has listed these in the biblical material section of his MTh dissertation, which you can read at http://carterclan. me.uk/dissertation.) In the New Testament, there are more instances of the word, especially the verb *chraomai* which means "to use, employ, make use of". But here's the thing: there are no occurrences of this verb—with the meaning "to use"—with a person as its object.

In other words, the Bible simply does not say, "God can use you", "God used me" or any other versions of this phrase. (The closest we come, which isn't very close, is in a couple of places where someone is described as "useful"—but not "useful to the Lord".)

What we do find in the New Testament are verses that contain the noun *skeuos*, which means "object, vessel, instrument". You're probably familiar with some of these verses which talk about God's people as "earthen vessels" or "pots".

A first impression of words like "vessel" and "instrument" might lead us to think that the Bible *is* referring to us as items of use—these things have a function, after all. But there are different ways of looking at items of pottery. When we look further, we will catch hold of a more enticing essence at the heart of these words, an essence woven through the delicate process of creation, crafting and care of these vessels.

HONOURED VESSELS

One of my favourite TV programmes of recent years is *The Great Pottery Throwdown*. Contestants are given various challenges: one week they are crafting vases on the potter's wheel and the next they're moulding elaborate bathroom suites, hoping the water doesn't drain out of the cracks formed during the firing process. What each piece has in common, though, is the thought and care the potters put in. Even when pressed for time, they want to imprint their creative stamp on their pieces—they want to honour the vessels they are making. I'm always struck by how fragile their creations are, how vulnerable and easily shattered during and after the process of crafting, firing and deco-rating. One of the delights of the *Throwdown* is the way the potters help us to see everyday items with new eyes: we appreciate the pieces all the more because of the intention of the creator.

I want to explore three passages of Scripture that involve analogies of pots without making the *functionality* of the pot the central point, giving us new ways to think about ourselves in relation to God.

LIGHT THROUGH THE CRACKS

Firstly, in 2 Corinthians 4, we are faced with the fragility of pots:

> But we have this treasure in jars of clay to show that
> this all-surpassing power is from God and not from us.
> *(2 Corinthians 4 v 7)*

Paul's readers would have been familiar with earthen vessels and clay jars in many different forms—especially with their inherent fragility as items made from clay, and their unimpressive appearance compared to vessels created for art and beauty. In this passage Paul is drawing a contrast between our frailty and the intense potency of the gospel. He is underlining the upside-down message we explored in the last chapter—God's power overthrowing the power systems of the world. It's this that Paul has in mind when he compares us to vessels.

The words that follow are loaded with hope all mixed up with raw honesty; they are words that have sustained Christians over centuries. We are hard-pressed, we are perplexed, we are persecuted—but we are not crushed. We are not abandoned (v 8-9). The point of Paul's comparison to vessels isn't about use; it's a picture of our weakness and

God's power. Paul is painting a great canvas of dynamic light blazing through fragile pots.

THE CREATOR'S HAND

When a potter begins to craft her pot on the wheel, the first thing she does, after adding water to soften the clay, is to make an opening in the pot. She plunges her hand into the very depths of the lump of clay, forming it, shaping it, moulding it. As the wheel keeps spinning, the potter works with the clay, inside and out. She, as the artist, can shape the clay as she wishes.

It's this kind of image that Paul has in mind in Romans 9:

> *But who are you, a human being, to talk back to God? "Shall what is formed say to the one who formed it, 'Why did you make me like this?'" Does not the potter have the right to make out of the same lump of clay some pottery for special purposes and some for common use? (Romans 9 v 20-21)*

Paul is referencing some familiar Old Testament imagery about potters and clay (Isaiah 29 v 16; 45 v 9) in order to help his readers consider the ways in which they are questioning the sovereignty of their Creator. Who are we, he is saying, to throw questions at God about how he has made us? God is the one who shaped and moulded us, the one who formed us in our mothers' wombs (Psalm 139 v 13). The incongruousness of a pot challenging its potter gives us pause to reflect on whether we kick back at what we might see as God's unfairness. Paul is referring to a specific example—the fact that some are saved and not others—but we can also draw a wider point here. God is God, and we are not. Just as a potter can choose what to do with clay, and that clay has no right to challenge the potter's intention, so God has sovereign choice over us.

This is where grace and mercy come crashing in, pounding through any arguments we might want to throw back. The amazing thing about God's saving plan is that it isn't anything to do with what we have done, or how useful we have been (Romans 9 v 16). It is simply to do with grace, freely given, and love that overcomes all the messes we make.

The potter has the right to squish the clay and chuck it away, if she wishes, and God could destroy us, too. But God *doesn't* (Jeremiah 18 v 6-8). And this is not all. As redeemed and loved children of God, we have not been grudgingly allowed into his kingdom, like wobbly plates of which God says "they'll do". We have been deliberately shaped for a beautiful purpose—set aside and prepared in advance for his glory (Romans 9 v 23). This imagery reminds us that we are weak, we are malleable, but also that we are crafted and shaped into God's image. Because of what Jesus has done for us, we are not destroyed; we are moulded with mercy and transformed with gentle and loving formation.

The focus in this passage isn't on the use of the vessels, but on the sovereignty of God. Just as the contestants of the *Throwdown* create their pieces with care and love, planning and smoothing and mending and transforming, so we are carefully crafted, chosen and accepted.

The problem with making this analogy of a pot and its creator a picture of God "using" us is that this kind of language actually limits God, squeezing out the truth of God's topsy-turvy priorities. It reduces him to a puppet-master, and it reduces us to tools instead of carefully crafted creations.

God does not love us because of what we do. God loves us because God loves us. And God wants to shape us to become more fully who we are created to be.

OBJECTS OF HONOUR

Finally, in 2 Timothy 2 v 20-21, we are transported into an analogy of pots in a large house. This seems to be the only example of how God might view an individual in terms of their use, so we need to explore it carefully.

> *In a large house there are articles not only of gold and silver, but also of wood and clay; some are for special purposes and some for common use. Those who cleanse themselves from the latter will be instruments for special purposes, made holy, useful to the Master and prepared to do any good work.*

In the 1st century, rich households possessed both common vessels and ones for more special, honoured purposes. Common pots were formed from poorer quality clay, made to be used and discarded. The Greek translation of the word for "common use" here is closer to "dishonourable", referring to vessels used for excrement or refuse. They were not made for long-term use or for displaying in the home.

The backdrop of this passage is a stark reminder to Timothy and the people of God to turn away from false teaching (v 14-19), with Paul drawing a direct parallel between these vessels of dishonour and false teachers ("the latter" in verse 21). The Greek translated "instruments for special purposes" in verse 21 is more literally "vessel for honour"—which throws a clearer light on words we might have taken to refer to our use as tools.

This is a passage full of wordplay. The key comparison is drawn not between items that are more and less useful, but between items that are honoured and beautiful and items that are disposable. Paul is calling us to more passionate discipleship and the pursuit of holiness. Just as an honoured vessel is useful to its master, so when we cleanse ourselves from sin and false teaching we become equipped for good works. Thinking of ourselves as honoured vessels in joyful and abandoned service to God is very different to living under a narrative of striving towards usefulness for usefulness' sake.*

A vessel is ready to be filled, and when we chase holiness we are filled, too, bursting out with God's glory and brimming with God's love. Just as the special items in the house were to be admired and were vital to the purposes of the master of the house, so we too are honoured and valued. Just as Timothy was encouraged to be fit for his ministry, we are called to free ourselves of all that holds us back, to strive for righteousness, to be effective partners in the gospel. And with our pursuit of holiness comes a new sense of joy, value and hope as we stand proudly in God's house, ready and willing to be part of his purposes.

God does not use us. Not in the sense of use that so diminishes and narrows us. Not in the sense of use that

---

* There are two other instances of this word "useful" in the New Testament, both used by Paul to describe individuals helping him in his ministry (2 Timothy 4 v 11 and Philemon 1 v 11). Notice that these do not describe the way God sees them, but are an expression of Paul's appreciation for them. Neither of them feature the verb "to use".

picks up and throws away. Not in the sense of use that sees us as tools rather than children of our Father.

When we describe God as a user, we become creatures of objectification rather than relationship.

THE HIGHLY FAVOURED ONE

All this talk of pots and vessels is a bit figurative so far. It's time to think about how to re-imagine our own stories in the light of what we have discovered about the biblical language of use.

One woman is perhaps most often of all spoken about in terms of her use to God. Perhaps we can free her—and us—from these bonds.

Look how God used Mary, just a young girl from a nowhere village. If God can use someone like that, he can definitely use someone like you!

These are the kinds of words we might have heard spoken about Mary the mother of Jesus. Yet the 19th-century Catholic theologian John Henry Newman spoke of Mary as a "Vessel of Honour", reminding us of Paul's illustration in 2 Timothy 2. This title remains in place in the Catholic community to this day. It seems to me that we can learn from this. We often find non-believers today viewing Mary's story through the "object of use" lens, and when they hear the "God used" language, it simply reiterates their narrative. God used a poor young girl to get what he wanted, they might say. What kind of God does that?

But when we look into Mary's story, we find something quite astonishing. We find Mary giving her consent—joyfully. "I am the Lord's servant ... May your word to me be fulfilled," she says (Luke 1 v 38).

Luke's report of a young woman using her own willing agency to partner with God is startling. A woman's wishes would not usually be worthy of comment in the culture. The 1st-century Jewish historian Josephus discounted the witness of women: "Let not the testimony of women be admitted, on account of the levity and boldness of their sex" (*Antiquities of the Jews*, book 4, section 219). Celsus, a 2nd-century critic of Christianity, mocked the idea of women as witnesses to the resurrection, calling them "hysterical females, deluded by sorcery". His statement is "consistent with the tendency in antiquity to see women as susceptible to religious madness", writes theologian Margaret McDonald in her book *Early Christian Women and Pagan Opinion* (p 109).

Mary's statement of her own intent stands out starkly against the thinking of the time. She was a pioneer for women, not only in her passion for God but in the example she gave us. She showed us that she was not, after all, an item to be used and discarded.

This becomes more evident still in the words of the Magnificat, Mary's song in response to God's work in her. It's a song that challenges cultural expectations as well as one that rejoices in the work of God in her life, speaking of a God who "brought down rulers from their thrones but has lifted up the humble", and "filled the hungry with good things but has sent the rich away empty" (Luke 1 v 52-53). Mary's song is bursting with signs of the upside-down kingdom that Jesus will uncover for everyone. It signifies the start of a lifelong relationship between Mary and her son—one of mutual love, trust and honour. It's no wonder that Mary's soul glorifies the Lord (v 46).

One of the things I love about Mary's story arc is the honour that Jesus bestows upon her, expressed in his care for her as he dies (John 19 v 26-27). Through a blur of agony, he pours out his love on her at the end, just as at the start, asking John to care for her as his mother.

What, then, can we say about Mary? How can we reframe her story into one of love and value rather than usefulness? Later in the book we're going to be exploring new ways in which we can reframe the language of use altogether. For now, though, would it be more accurate to say that her story is one of partnership, of willing agency, of mutual love? And can we apply this to our own lives, too?

Are we ready to move beyond being used?

A NEW LOVE STORY

Let's re-imagine our love story with God as one in which we love and are loved to the full, rather than a place in which we must perform. Instead of living under words of utility and productivity, we are called to places of wild abandon and grand adventure. Like Mary, we are vessels of honour, lovingly crafted by the Creator's hand, honoured and sanctified. We are jars of clay, frail yet blazing with holy light.

Let's not fall into the trap of thinking that the desire of God's heart is to get his children to do things for him. God's heart is for intimacy and transformation. God speaks to us in the language of love, calling us forward, speaking soothing words over us and drawing us into the knowledge of who we really are.

Arise, my darling,
My beautiful one, come with me.

See! The winter is past;
The rains are over and gone.
Flowers appear on the earth;
The season of singing has come.

(Song of Songs 2 v 10-12)

Perhaps you feel stuck in perpetual winter, heavy in the bonds of uselessness or the desperation to be useful. Perhaps you feel like broken pottery, shattered on the floor around you. Hear God calling you today. Hear the echoes of a new season of singing, where you are no longer merely useful, but loved and called deeper into a meaningful and consensual partnership with the God of the universe. Hear words that can mend and reshape, words that draw you to new frontiers where joy is abundant and peace cascades through all your fractures.

FOR PRAYER & REFLECTION

Father, I praise you that you love me because of who I am,
Created in your image,
Not because of what I do for you.
Thank you for the freedom of knowing that you are not a user,
Not an exploiter.
You are the God of creation
And the God of perfect love.
Draw me into deeper holiness,
That I may be fit for your purposes,
And ready to dance into joyful partnership.
Amen.

- Think about the language around "God uses". What experience have you had with this kind of language? How do you feel about it now?

- Reflect on Mary's story and her song in Luke 1. How would you describe her partnership with God, and her story of honour and love?

4. A Church
for Broken People

It's church coffee time again. I'm unwell with another infection, struggling to stand. "How are you?" someone says, smiley and warm. "Are you better now?"

"I'm fine, thanks," I say, and smile back at them as if saying the words makes it true, knowing deep down I have chosen once again to mask my pain. I don't want to annoy people, or turn them away, or seem like the whinger in the corner. So I conceal my reality with the mask of fine, and add another brick to my wall of vulnerability.

Coffee time can be difficult for even the most gregarious of people. It can often be a time when the useless narrative is increased within us—we feel we ought to be displaying success in our Christian lives, yet underneath is a wide-open chasm of yearning for authenticity.

We've just reflected on how we sometimes build a narrative of having to be useful to God, and how the "God using" language can exacerbate the uneasiness deep within us. The problem is that we stay bowed under this load even in places where we should be free to express the truth. To challenge this narrative, in these next three chapters we are

LIZ CARTER

going to look more closely and practically at God's view of
weakness and usefulness, exploring three ways in which the
productivity lie can seep into our faith and affect both our
relationship with God and our view of self. And then we're
going to see how the truth of God's upside-down kingdom
plays out in our specific circumstances.

The first has to do with church.

In Alia Joy's poignant book *Glorious Weakness*, Alia, who
suffers from a number of physical and mental illnesses,
recalls how she felt forced to pretend she was ok when faced
with the question "How are you?" in church:

> *My tongue was long trained by Sunday School
> etiquette and polite society never to cough up
> unpalatable words like depression or suicide or
> antidepressant in church company. Instead, "fine"
> became my answer. (p 173)*

Alia felt forced into a box which hurt too much to open.
It was only later, when she had lived under her mask for a
long time, that she realised people were actually starving for
honesty and vulnerability. "When I first wrote the words
'bipolar disorder' on my blog, I was terrified. What would
people think?" But it was as she began to write honestly
about faith and mental illness that people started to connect
with her. "The emails started coming in" (p 19).

I wonder if you can identify with this "mask of fine".
Are you unable to share freely because you feel you don't
measure up to others, or you think you won't be heard? The
truth is, those who appear more successful or "useful" are
probably wearing that mask, too, aching to share their own

pain but holding back behind those bland and futile words: "I'm fine, thanks. How are you?"

When we say those words, we close doors and evade more meaningful conversation. Inside us there might be a whole ocean of desolation, but once again we suppress it, we paste on a smile (Christians should always be happy, after all…) and we go home with our heads hung low and our eyes burning with tears.

I know that I can get so caught up in my own sense of failure and comparison that I forget to notice my friend who is hiding her own pain behind her own mask of fine. The truth is that so many of us carry our burdens around with us. We long to share them, but instead we keep on raising our defences and slinking further down into our own sense of worthlessness. (Claire Musters' wonderful and honest book *Taking off the Mask* can help you explore this idea further.)

In this chapter, then, we're going to think about how we can transform church communities into places where honesty is possible when we value one another. We're going to begin to think outside the box of use and break free into the joy of being honoured—and vital—as part of the body of Christ.

First of all, what about those times when "honoured and vital" seems to be reserved for the Most Useful People?

THE VERY USEFUL FAMILY

Louise had thought long and hard about going. She'd screwed up her courage and tidied herself up—as much as she could, anyway. She knew she needed a shower. But she just didn't have the energy, and besides, she couldn't pay the electricity bill this month.

Church was a beacon to her, though. She'd had a few drinks already, the only way she could get through the day, but surely she'd be welcomed there anyway?

She sat at the back. She'd stay for the service and then go. But then they mentioned coffee, cakes and community, and Louise was so hungry. So lonely.

In the hall a large mass of people milled around, whispering and laughing in little groups. A shiny young family stood in the centre, surrounded by smiling people. Their two well-behaved children stood meekly by their mother's side, staring round with wide eyes.

Louise hugged her arms around herself, overwhelmed by the noise and the weight of loneliness that lodged in her chest like a physical pain. Someone nearby distracted her. "They're new," he was saying. "Apparently he's an architect."

The woman next to him smiled. "Wow. Must be God's provision for the extension project!"

"Yeah. And his wife, she's a teacher, and you know we need more leaders in children's church."

The woman smiled larger. "Think how God could use her here! And look at those children. Angelic! Just what we need to model some good behaviour to the kids round here."

Louise watched as the two of them made their way through the crowd to shake the new couple's hands. "What a lovely welcome," the man said. His wife nodded and smiled, too, and the air was full of happy greetings. *Do you want to come to our welcome dinner? Do you need any help with settling into your new home? We can send a party to paint, garden, anything you need.*

Louise cradled her mug of lukewarm coffee close. There was a space around her and it echoed with loud accusations.

She thought about how her tiny flat so desperately needed painting. Then she thought about how her own child wasn't angelic at all.

Then Louise turned around and slunk out of the hall, without anyone saying a word to her. On the way out she overheard the vicar talking to his wife. "Make sure you welcome that new family. Sounds like they could be really useful to us."

BROKEN PEOPLE WELCOME HERE

I wonder if you have ever felt like Louise. Maybe you have been the one sitting at the back, afraid you will not be welcome. Maybe you have been the one hanging on the edges during coffee time, hoping someone will notice you, talk to you, speak more than platitudes to you. Or maybe you know that on the outside you look like one of the shiny ones—impressive, talented, *useful*; but you've lost your temper yet again with the kids on the way to church, and you know you're not really very shiny at all.

Maybe you have felt useless in church.

This sense of uselessness can be intensified by the idea that there is some kind of standard we should measure up to as Christians. When congregation members applaud and acclaim the useful people, others can feel ignored and even unwanted. We might feel that we often see excitement surrounding the gifted folk, but only rarely hear such a buzz around the homeless man who has nothing to offer but a lingering odour, or the elderly lady who comes along intermittently because some weeks she feels up to it and other weeks needs to stay home. We might feel that we were loved when we were useful, once upon a time, but since The Thing happened—the diagnosis, the bereavement, the breakdown, the divorce—there's no place for us in church anymore.

One quick glance at any of the Gospels is enough to show that Jesus took the opposite approach. Jesus stopped for the ceremonially unclean and listened to those with disabilities. He touched the lepers, had tea with a tax collector and welcomed prostitutes and thieves. When we become more like Jesus, we defy the harmful narrative of the world around us.

What if we imitated the earliest church, where, as Nick Page writes, "Christians welcomed those at the bottom of the heap. More than welcomed: empowered" (*Kingdom of Fools*)? The great news about church is that when it is doing what it should, it can be a place that breaks down walls and reverses the story, a place where we practise radical grace and generosity. A place where we welcome Louise, then organise a flat-painting party.

A BODY OF HONOUR

Jesus' revolutionary attitude towards those whom society discounts is perfectly expressed in Paul's metaphor of the body of Christ in 1 Corinthians 12. We've already explored Paul's reframing of wisdom and power in 1 Corinthians 1, and now we find God continuing to reverse that cultural narrative, transforming the ethos of a fledgling group of believers.

In the ancient world, the notion of "the body" as a collection of members wasn't new. Greek and Roman philosophers and politicians used this analogy to illustrate the hierarchical order of society, with the emperor at the

head and the citizens as the other members of the body—
calling it the "body politic". Some members were held as
more important than others, and so should be treated as
such; some were less important, even dispensable.

The weaker members, viewed in terms of what they could
do to serve the whole, were compared to the hidden parts
of a human body—perceived as vulgar and dirty. The jobs
done by the weaker members of the body were fit only for
people who already had a lowly status in society.

Paul's picture of the body not only undermines this
analogy but blows it wide apart. "God has placed the parts
in the body, every one of them, just as he wanted them to
be," he writes (v 18), and then goes on to proclaim—in
biting contrast to the usual imagery his audience would
have been familiar with—that those parts of the body seen
as weaker are, in fact, indispensable, and "the parts that
we think are less honourable we treat with special honour"
(v 22-23).

Paul is not only speaking against the prevailing culture
but into the heart of what is going on in the Corinthian church. The Corinthians have fallen into the trap of
reflecting some of the more damaging norms in their
society. In the previous verses, Paul has been reprimand-
ing the church for their careless approach to the act of
Communion (11 v 17-33). They are approaching the table
without thought, some stuffing themselves while others go
hungry. This sloppy approach to Communion underpins
other ways in which the Corinthian church think of and
treat members. Worship is chaotic and harmful (11 v 17),
with certain gifts elevated over others (14 v 20-23, 26-33),
and certain people are seen as superior while others are

inferior or even useless (12 v 23). In fact, the church has taken on the exact thinking of the philosophers and orators of their age (3 v 1; 10 v 23-24).

But Paul cuts through the prevailing arrogance that is so toxic to a brand-new group of believers. What Paul does, in his new and enticing interpretation of the church as the body, is to set the picture so starkly against old understandings that it shatters every prejudice, exposing any self-serving within the body. God is breathing new life and a powerful new subculture into being: the weaker are treated with special honour (12 v 23), and each part should have equal concern towards one another (v 25).

Paul ends this section with a striking picture of how the body works together, each part affecting each others. "If one part suffers, every part suffers with it; if one part is honoured, every part rejoices with it" (v 26). I know how this feels. Sometimes, when I am in acute pain, my chest clamped in a vice, I feel crushed, as though every part of me will shatter into tiny pieces. Pain rushes through my back, down my arms and my legs, even into my toes—a whole-body scream of agony. Every part of me is locked into suffering because one part of my body is sick.

Another day, I'm at the top of a mountain. The landscape is radiant with light and beauty. Elation rushes through my body, capturing me from head to toe, zinging through my fingers and singing in my soul. Every part of me is liberated into joy while one part of my body revels in this captivating view.

Paul says the body of Christ is like that. Frail and vibrant, suffering and rejoicing with one another, woven through with sparks of joy and aching with unspeakable sadness; we are most together in Christ when every single member is honoured.

BELONGING TO ONE ANOTHER

In Romans 12, Paul draws this vivid picture again, this time emphasising belonging:

> *For just as each of us has one body with many members ... each member belongs to all the others.*
>
> *(v 4-5)*

Within the body we are connected to one another: we rely on one another within our weaknesses, and lend our strengths to other members who are weaker. Within this body there is a life-flow that reflects God's glorious purpose in allowing weakness to become strength, and strength to become a lot less important than we might think.

I often wonder how this body would function, here on earth, if we all lived in wholeness and perfection—if God answered all our prayers as we wished. Without weakness, we would have no need of reliance on each other. We wouldn't, in fact, look much like a body at all; we would become complacent in our individualism, mired more deeply in self. "I'm good on my own, thanks," the foot would say to the knee; "I've no need of you. Leave me alone."

It just wouldn't work, would it? Because we need every part. We need the weak as much as the strong, the unimpressive as much as the attractive, the broken as much as the whole.

This image reminds us that frailty doesn't mean failure. Paul wanted the early church to grasp something shockingly radical about God's kingdom priorities, something with a fragrance so sweet that it brings healing where there is brokenness and hope where there is despair. We, though we are many, form one body (Romans 12 v 5), and that body is palpably real and beautiful at the same time, bursting at the seams with uselessness and fragility, heaving with mourning and sadness and joy and kindness all at the same time. When the heart is hurting, the hands are holding. When the knees are tired, the feet speak encouragement.

This picture of the church is alluring and hopeful, and it calls to us within our own struggles and feelings of uselessness. Think back for a moment to those painful coffee times where the mask goes on and the words stay inside, where you feel alone and unheard. Then think about a new culture, where the upside down prevails and belonging is not defined by what we are able to offer but by our God-breathed humanity and dignity. It's a culture that requires vulnerability, where through our sharing of the raw edges of our deepest selves and our willingness to carry the burdens of others around us, we find this picture of the body of Christ to be more than a beguiling whisper. When we take off our masks, we are helping to create the kind of church culture that Paul—and Jesus—envisaged.

And as we reflect on what it would mean to share more freely of our own frailty, we will become more aware of those around us. Many people have been living in a broken place when it comes to church, feeling far from valued and far from vital. What if we turned this around? What if we plunged into the Upside Down—and held their weary hands as we jumped?

LOST AND FOUND IN LOCKDOWN

Lynn has lived with multiple sclerosis for many years. She has been using a wheelchair since 2014, a diagnosis of arthritis adding to her daily struggle. Some of her church experience as a young person was difficult—suffering with epilepsy, she was told that she must be demon-possessed, and that she should flush away her medication. In the last few years, she has felt isolated from church, not due to deliberate exclusion but simply because she often hasn't had the mobility to get to church and sit through a service.

During lockdown, as our church began to offer online services, many people like Lynn began to find a new community of faith and belonging. While some were feeling lost and adrift in this "new normal", many disabled people were discovering a new kind of inclusion. For Lynn, it was a joy to be part of something, a place where she could grow in faith, and worship with others. It wasn't only that, though.

When we asked Lynn if she'd be interested in being on the PCC (the lay leadership of the church), she was thrilled. Zoom was opening up new possibilities like never before. Her confidence grew and so did the opportunities; she took part in services by sending in videos of prayers and readings, got involved with the food bank and the diocesan disability training, and headed up a new eco-church committee, revolutionising the way the church approached matters of energy, justice and climate change. For Lynn, it wasn't that she suddenly found herself useful, but that she found herself an honoured, valued and vital member of the body. She was no longer hidden away at home, feeling that her weakness made her useless. She came to see that she was as much part of our body, within her weakness, as everyone else—and that we needed her.

One of the reasons that she, and I, found this to be such a powerful season in the way we viewed ourselves, was the culture of authenticity and vulnerability that was developed by the people coming together in these online spaces. We shared deeply of ourselves—and we were heard.

WHEN CHURCH GETS PAUL'S MEMO

We want more.

We want to lay ourselves out in stark honesty, without worry of judgment or negativity. We yearn for a community of people who epitomise the body as Paul described it, a place we can safely bare our souls and bear one another's burdens. Jesus' words and Paul's thoughts all point towards a new community of openness and accountability, where weaker members are celebrated and struggling members supported. A community where people are not seen through the lens of what they contribute and do, but as people to love.

The fragrance of the Holy Spirit weaves through this kind of community, invading the ground with God's grace, reconciliation and unconditional love. When we fail to be that community, we fail to express church as church was intended, and we fail one another. But when churches welcome broken people, when we embrace Louise and Lynn and all those who fear they are too weak to be part of the body of Christ, we are demonstrating the kingdom of God in all its inside-out expansiveness.

How can we ensure that every person in our churches knows that they are valued and vital? My church has five values, with two focused on looking outward: Loving our neighbours and loving each other. Within these values, we have defined several key words and phrases that we aim towards:

Forgiveness. Humility. Kindness. Encouragement. Listening. Talking to each other and not about each other. Acceptance. Welcome. Hospitality. Reconciliation.

These words may seem commonplace on their own, but together they spark with revolutionary power, and when they are applied within the spirit of Paul's counter-cultural picture of the body of Christ, they are explosive. Perhaps these are words we can all reflect on in order to write new stories in our own homes and churches.

Many of us *are* trying our best, as individuals and as churches. Many of us intentionally try to create an ethos of welcome and inclusiveness, aware of the way people can feel minimised and ignored within church communities. We can't always get it right, because we are human, but we can try. And our trying might help one person feel a little less broken than before.

Paul envisaged a body where unity finds expression in the dignity and value of each member, a place where we are dazzled by the bride of Christ in all her radiant splendour, an explosion of grace and mutual care, an earthly reminder that love never fails. What a joy it is when we embrace this picture, celebrating church as a place that can flip the script.

FOR PRAYER & REFLECTION

Jesus, when I am steeped in my frailty,
Remind me that my strength is found in you.
When I am far from fine,
Give me a community of care
Where I may fling my mask aside
And express the pain that seethes within.
When I feel dishonoured,
May I know that you shower me in love without
conditions.
May I extend this unconditional welcome to all those
around me,
And paint your picture of a body of honour.
Amen.

- Take some time in the coming week to read through 1 Corinthians 11 – 13, asking God to speak into your heart about kingdom priorities.

- How did Louise's story make you feel? Do you think that your church has an ethos of welcoming all, or are the useful people more noticed? What steps could you take to welcome broken people into your church?

5. A New Kind
of Wholeness

She stands on the stage, smiling wide and bouncing with energy. "Since God healed me," she says, "you wouldn't believe how much he has used me. I've achieved so much more for the kingdom in a body that actually works!"

I wonder if you, like me, have ever heard this kind of thing and thought, "I know I am God's beloved child. But… I'd be more useful if I were more whole."

The world around us pushes a message of self-improvement leading to usefulness and productivity: getting ourselves healthy, shedding our baggage, bettering ourselves, optimising our earning power. If we are not improving, we won't be as useful.

And this lie infects our faith. What if we still long to be "fixed" because somewhere deep down we still believe God values usefulness more than weakness—that the people who will change the world for Jesus are the healthy, sorted-out ones, and that those are the ones God loves the best? What if we really think we are only going to get useful when we are whole?

I want to explore with you a new kind of wholeness. One that does not depend on the state of health of our minds and bodies, but that blooms within our brokenness.

An upside-down kind of wholeness.

WORDS THAT WOUND

Tracy Williamson, a Christian author who is deaf, told me about a time she heard some words about usefulness that nearly broke her.

As a brand-new Christian, she was invited to a special intercession meeting at her church, where it was declared that God was going to heal people that evening. Tracy was called to the front. Being such a new Christian, she wasn't sure how to respond as they laid hands on her ears and prayed, repeating "Jesus" into her ears to test if she was yet hearing.

For two hours.

"They were determined to see me healed," she told me. "I tried with all my might to step into being someone who could hear. They commanded my ears to be open, they cast out spirits of deafness and released hearing into my ears."

Tracy was exhausted and overwhelmed, their shouts and commands a "discordant cacophony" jarring all around her in harsh and painful waves. At the end of the two hours, she was still deaf. And that's when one of the elders said to her, "Tracy, you must have more faith, because God won't be able to use you as a deaf person."

"His words stunned me," Tracy told me. "They went straight to my heart like an arrow and cut me deep." She had tried so hard to believe that healing would come, struggling through those two intimidating hours, and now she was left in despair. "I had disappointed God with my

VALUABLE

lack of faith, and he would not be able to use me. I was
devastated."

She felt a deep sense of shame, many of the negative beliefs
she had formed because of a painful childhood churning in
her head once again. "I believed I was an inferior Christian,
second rate, both because of my disability and my lack of
faith. I withdrew into myself, feeling there was no point in
being enthusiastic about God and my Christian life if he
couldn't use me."

As time went by, those words cut an ever-deepening
wound inside of her. Then she met the gospel singer/song-
writer Marilyn Baker, who is blind, and they became great
friends. Marilyn knew that God didn't see her blindness as
an inferiority, and that God worked alongside her, within
her disability, to touch countless lives. Her attitude had a
profound effect on Tracy, and, as she became assured of
God's love, acceptance and partnership with her, she was
transformed.

One night Marilyn invited Tracy to share her testimony at one of her concerts. Tracy was terrified, with all the
old words flinging accusations at her; but as she shared
about God's deep healing in her life, people were touched,
restored, and brought to Christ. "I was full of awe and joy,"
Tracy says. "I realised the words the elder had spoken had
been totally false. God would never reject me for being deaf
and in fact would turn my weakness to his glory."

Tracy forgave the elder, but still wishes she had never
heard those words. "Our words have great power to either
build up or destroy," she says.

~~GET WHOLE TO BE USEFUL~~
BE BROKEN AND VALUED

Tracy's story (you can read more of it in her book *The Father's Kiss*) echoes my own experience, and, sadly, the experience of others who have been bruised and scarred by words and actions like these. It's often people with the most obvious problems—whether physical, practical or emotional—who are targeted for sometimes very aggressive prayer. But it's not only the huge issues in our lives that lend themselves to the feeling that we would be better if we were whole; it's all the small things. It's when someone's stutter means they can't find the courage to tell others about Jesus. It's when they're too exhausted to make it to a church event—yet again. It's when you feel as though you're failing at parenting, and it's when you feel like you just need to snap out of your sadness. All these issues pile upon one another, building a great tower of uselessness and hopelessness; we can never get fixed, we think. We can never be sorted out enough to be helpful to God.

Sometimes, of course, making positive changes in our lives is healthy and important to our growth as human beings and as Christians. But when the natural progression of growth gets all tangled up with the forced expectations of productivity and use, and the idea that the better we become, the more useful we are, the good growth can slow down, choked by thorny negative growth.

In this chapter I want to reframe the idea that we must be whole to be useful. Not only should we throw out the "useful" part of that idea, but also the "whole"—when used to mean "mended". What if we could fling that notion aside and be released into the liberty of discovering God's power *within* our brokenness? What if instead of looking for usefulness in wholeness, we find a new and more dynamic power in God's weakness-powered wholeness?

THE CELESTIAL VENDING MACHINE

By this point in the book, you've probably easily spotted one misunderstanding at the heart of Tracy's story: the assumption that our use to God is the most important thing to God. But there's another misunderstanding here, too: the certainty that God is here to make everything better for us in the here and now. That misunderstanding is often supported with cherry-picked Scripture that doesn't take account of the weakness and foolishness at the heart of the kingdom of God. It is born in the idea that God loves us, and so wants us to be whole.

God does love us. God does want us to be whole. But this doesn't mean that we can somehow escape difficulty in our lives, or that God protects us from scars—or even great deep dark wounds. It means that one day, ultimately, we will find full wholeness and joy in God's presence. We live in the *now and the not-yet*, with the *now* all laden with weariness and strife, and the *not-yet* igniting sustaining hope in the centre of it all. Sometimes, we do get glimpses of what will, one day, be our entire reality: we plunge deep into great roaring waterfalls of love and joy, and then we take those moments onward through the trudge of now, the imprint of those drops of not-yet still sprinkling our heads and our hearts.

But the not-yet is just that: not yet. The misunderstanding about being "fixed" comes from the belief that we are entitled to all the good and all the healing right now, and that God will give us what we want when we use the correct currency, just like a vending machine that responds to our wishes when we post the right coins into the slot. The correct currency, in this story, is our faith, and if we don't get what we want, we're not doing it right. We don't have enough of it. When we're told that, it wounds us deeply and twists our stories of our journeys with God. God is the giver, but we are not enough. God is all-powerful, but our weakness is getting in the way.

But that is not the story that Scripture tells us, and it doesn't have to be our story.

A LIFE IN DANGER
Take some time now to read 2 Corinthians 11 v 23-30, and reflect on Paul's painful experiences.

Imprisoned, flogged, exposed to death.

Beaten with rods, pelted with stones.

Shipwrecked and left floundering in open seas.

In danger from rivers, bandits, Jews and Gentiles, false believers.

In danger in the city, in the country, at sea.

Burnt out, exhausted, hungry, thirsty, cold and naked.

Paul was speaking into a situation in Corinth where false teachers who called themselves apostles were pushing a different gospel—a message which led them to boast in themselves and their own achievements (v 12-15). Paul, hesitant to boast in himself, listed his own credentials of weakness to counterbalance their boasting in strength (v 18). He encouraged the Corinthians to reject these worldly ways of thinking and to find their strength elsewhere. The Corinthian Christians who had signed up to these false teachings must have found Paul's words both unsettling and foolish, because, in their view, the sort of hardships he listed pointed to a gospel without power and success. They wanted something to boast in; they wanted wholeness, they wanted success. But Paul knew that this not only contradicted the heart of the gospel but also brought emptiness and shattering failure when bad things happened.

Paul did not escape suffering. His circumstances were, in fact, often dire, even deadly, as he took the gospel to new frontiers, risking his life and health. And he not only lived this troublesome life but saw it as an integral part of discipleship; something to take pride in, rather than boasting in riches, health and achievement (2 Corinthians 4 v 1-12).

Ultimately, Paul viewed all these things in the light of future glory. His expectant hope for eternity, where all weakness, mourning, pain and sadness will come to an end, gave him courage within his troubles, and so he did not lose heart: "Though outwardly we are wasting away, yet inwardly we are being renewed day by day" (2 Corinthians 4 v 16).

Reflecting on these words in the light of the stories we often live within, fed by society's political, social and economic models, we find God's Upside Down invading our ground. We begin to see ourselves not as people deserving of everything we want, but as beloved children who find consolation in our Father's arms—children who might not have perfect lives, but who live within the profound and healing depths of holy foolishness, assured by the hope of glory. One day, we will be immersed in all that it means to be perfectly whole, where chains are broken and freedom reigns.

WHERE GOD'S POWER IS DISPLAYED

Weakness, then, is here to stay—until Jesus comes again. But it's not just something to put up with. Weakness is a place where we experience God's power, and a place where God's power is displayed to others around us, too. And so weakness can be a place of flourishing.

In 2 Corinthians 12 v 7-10 Paul writes of his "thorn"—some kind of physical or mental infirmity. Paul sees it as a reminder to avoid any conceit about his own power and any complacency about God's work in him. He pleads with God to take it away, but God says to him, "My grace is sufficient for you, for my power is made perfect in weakness." Paul tells us that he will therefore boast even more gladly about his weaknesses, so that Christ's power may rest on him (v 9).

We can appreciate Paul's meaning more fully when we explore some of the Greek words in this passage. *Arkei*, which is translated "is sufficient", means "to be enough", with a flavour of *more* than enough—it suggests contentment and satisfaction. The grace of Christ is plentiful for us in our weakness as we become strong by his might, not ours. *Dynamis*, which is translated "power", is the root of our word "dynamite"—reminding us to keep celebrating the incredible fact that God's explosive, universe-crafting power is expressed in our weakness. Finally, *episkenose*—translated "rest", as in "so that Christ's power may rest on me", literally means "to tent upon": in other words, to pitch one's tent upon, to dwell among, to abide with. Paul knows that Christ's power isn't unreachable but is here among us. We see God, experience God and encounter God more clearly in our weakness.

Paul's understanding of weakness is rooted in all his upside-down thinking about kingdom reversals. He understands that weakness lies at the very heart of the gospel, with Jesus dying in agony, and that there is a mystery behind this weakness that reveals God's nature to us: powerful, gracious, loving and self-sacrificial. This is a mystery to us because in our human reasoning we cannot grasp the paradox of a God of power and Christ on the cross. And it's a mystery to us because we think that power is about strength, yet Paul tells us that it is perfected in weakness. We somehow think that God must need us to be strong for him, forgetting that God again and again chooses to work within the confines of weakness. It's mind-blowing, and yet deeply consoling, to know that God's saving plan is rooted in extreme human frailty.

We might believe that God will only change the world through the mended people. Yet what we are seeing here is that the most glorious display of God's power isn't actually to be found in superhuman Christians changing the world, but in God's superhuman power, most clearly seen in our weaknesses. And that is a new kind of wholeness. Here, we are not forced to try to bring pain and weakness to a close, fearing being branded a failure if we do not. We are called instead to intimacy with the Creator of the universe *within* that place of weakness.

THE HEAVENLY FLIP

I was undone.

I had nothing left. I had begged God to release me from pain, and I still hurt. I went to the meeting bowed over; longing to worship but broken and shattered. How could

I ever be useful to God, I thought, if I kept on getting sick? How could my testimony help others if I never got whole?

I sat through the time of worship, hugging my arms around me, miserable and disengaged.

It was one particular song that crashed through the barriers and took me into encounter. It was a song that spoke of God being everything to us, in all of life, in the good and bad, the storms and the sunshine. The simple line "God in my hurting" halted me in my misery-tracks and jolted me awake.

God in my hurting. Suddenly I was flooded with liquid love. The molten gold of it did not melt my pain, but it took me deeper into an encounter forged in weakness, an encounter all the more profound for that weakness. I was still undone, but I was undone in deep awareness of the presence of Christ. I was undone in everlasting arms.

When we insist on our interpretation of wholeness as a God-given right, we lose something precious, something that sustains us when we are broken: a place of intense intimacy. Weakness can be a place to encounter God—a place we learn to depend on God's power, not our own.

How do we live in this paradox in everyday life? The now and the not-yet, the weariness and the peace, the pain and the encounter? How do we change our narratives so that we live in the assurance that we don't have to be mended for God to work with us and through us, while finding the courage to celebrate the times God breaks through in power?

I've heard the phrase "the heavenly flip" to describe our response to God's upside-down kingdom. When we are struggling, we flip perspective—we suffer, "and yet" we still praise (Psalm 42 v 11). We do the heavenly flip when we need to apply the Upside Down to our own lives.

In times of weakness, we become more keenly aware of our need for God, and so turn to more fervent prayer. We may not always experience God's power tangibly, but we can be assured that God holds us where we are, comforting us through Scripture, through the whisper of the Spirit, through the words of others. It's when we struggle that we realise we are not created to do this all on our own. We reach out to God when we can do nothing apart from him (John 15 v 5), and we lean on God when our legs are too shaky to hold us up on their own. Weakness can be a time we reach out to others more, too, allowing ourselves to depend on them as we live out what it means to be part of the body of Christ in all its ragged glory. And weakness shines a spotlight on what true wholeness will look like, by emphasising our need for God and so calling us to holy yearning—which fires us into passionate prayer.

We have a challenge, then, in the light of this gospel of wholeness-in-weakness. We have a responsibility to make changes in our own churches, our own homes, our own relationships—changes that will lead to transformation and soul-healing. Perhaps we need to make changes to the stories we live within, stories about God granting all our wishes and (as we'll see in the next chapter) about how God causes and uses our pain, because these things are built on flimsy ground and then implode when real life invades. Perhaps we need to embrace God's gracious saving work through the brokenness rather than insisting on God's compliance in making everything better—acknowledging that certainty and wholeness are part of the not-yet, and while we live here in the now we must accept and embrace the ambiguity we find ourselves in.

Maybe that's when those of us who feel useless, in any sense at all, will feel liberated from the burden of failure and find ourselves immersed in new stories that surge with joy: contentment in acceptance, truth that liberates, grace that covers sin and love that still loves in pain.

THE WEAKNESS OF JESUS

Looking for usefulness in wholeness leads to us missing out on the depths of a God who has walked the farthest shores of pain for us. The writer to the Hebrews reminds us that "We do not have a high priest who is unable to empathize with our weaknesses, but we have one who has been tempted in every way, just as we are—yet he did not sin" (Hebrews 4 v 15), and that because of this, we can "approach God's throne of grace with confidence" (v 16). These "weaknesses" encompass all the struggles and suffering we could ever experience—in mind, in body, in spirit. Jesus experienced them, too.

Those wild edges of weakness were still written on Jesus' body even after the resurrection, when he showed his wounds to Thomas (John 20 v 27). Thomas was filled with awe: "My Lord and my God!" he said in an encounter born in doubt and yet sealed in scarred truth. And it's the same for us; when we encounter the love of Jesus in our weakness-tinted wholeness, we find freedom and hope. Because Jesus knew extreme weakness and frailty, we can be confident we are safe in love that doesn't just spring from words but from bitter and wounding experience.

And Jesus' raw weakness is still stronger than the greatest strength we can muster in ourselves.

When you are weak, you are strong. You may not feel strong; you may feel as though strength is a distant memory. But here's the thing: Jesus felt that, too. And now he's with you, by the Spirit. Now he's abiding in your pit.

Now he's tenting on you.

FOR PRAYER & REFLECTION

Jesus, your wounds have set me free
And yet they linger on, stark and ragged,
Displaying the weakness at the heart of your kingdom.
When I grasp for a mended life,
Sit with me in the broken pieces.
When I feel useless in my pain,
Take me to new places where wholeness means hope.
Write a new freedom-story around my life,
And may I write it with those around me.
Amen.

• Do you identify with the idea of God as a celestial vending machine? How does that sit with you when life hurts?

• Have you ever felt that you need to be "fixed" before God can work in and through you? Why do you think this is? Reflect on Tracy's story and think about the words that bound her and then the words that set her free.

6. A New
Hope Story

"We're throwing you a book launch party," my friends said.

My first book, *Catching Contentment*, was about to be published, something I'd dreamed of for so long. The book had been written through and because of long-term illness and pain, and I felt like I *deserved* this. My friends decorated the hall, and over a hundred friends and relatives from all over the country were set to come.

But then I caught double pneumonia.

Instead of reading from my new book and drinking champagne with my friends, I lay in a hospital bed, struggling to breathe. Instead of celebrating this achievement in my life, I was tangled in IV lines and quivering with pain.

The party went ahead without me. People told me that it was all the more poignant for my absence, given the subject of the book, which explores what it means to find contentment when life hurts. But I just felt bitter and sad.

People were full of compassion and love, and their support helped me through. But there were one or two statements made during that time that sent me back into a murky old narrative. "God is using you so much more *because* of your illness," went the gist of it.

The thing is, on one level I knew they were right, in the spirit of the words. God was turning the situation to good and bringing others closer to him, the words of my book somehow taking on more profound power within the circumstances. But for me, in the hospital bed, the "using" language was not enough. This language failed me in the midst of actual pain. It reduced my agony to a tool and my suffering to a means to an end. It turned my sadness and disappointment into self-indulgent emotions that should not matter because I was being *useful*.

I did find God in that hospital bed. I found Jesus sitting by my side, dwelling in the despair with me. I found him where his own wounds still gape, in depths he plumbed for me and in nails he bore for me. I found him in the consolation of the Spirit and the compassion of those around me.

But I didn't turn to him and smile bravely, thanking him for using me in my adversity.

IF I CAN'T GET FIXED...

In the previous chapter, we reflected on our pursuit of usefulness within the context of healing and wholeness. We thought about how God works in and through us in the deep cracks of the long wait for wholeness. But, leading on from that knowledge, it's easy to slip into a new false narrative, one that goes like this:

> *I know that everything doesn't have to be wonderful in my life in order for God to work in me or for me*

*to witness to others about God's love. But that's ok,
because God works in adversity, right? God uses my
suffering. I keep hearing stories of people who have
experienced tragedies in their lives, but God uses them
to help others. So, I ought to be able to deal with any
weakness, because at least I feel like it has some kind
of purpose. At least I know it's not all in vain.*

The problem is that pain leaves us in a heap of weariness where words about the use of that pain can become
burdens that weigh us down even more. There are two
damaging assertions that spring from this "at least I can be
useful" narrative, both of which belittle and minimise our
pain and give us twisted ideas about God's purpose and
love for us.

*1. If I can be useful in my weakness, I shouldn't feel bad
about it.*
We often extol people who suffer. "Look what good has
come about from their pain," we say. "They're so inspir-
ing." Sometimes these kinds of remarks lead people to feel
as though they should play down their suffering and hide
the wounds they have gathered along the way. Instead, they
must swallow back the tears and smile, they must say it was
all worth it; they must not lament their losses.

While it is true that God works beauty from ashes, the
journey can be painful, and the destination does not mean
that the pain never happened. When I gave birth to my
children I was elated, but this did not lessen the reality of
the intense pain I had lived.

2. If I can be useful in my weakness, God must be content to see me suffer.

The second problem is the idea that because God works in and through our difficulties (Romans 8 v 28), it must mean that God dispassionately designs and enforces them for his own ends, and so must be unmoved by our struggles and our pain. This leads us to think that he doesn't really care about us as individuals—we're just a kind of tool that he's chosen to bend out of shape in order to bring use from it.

We forget that the Bible allows for ambiguity when it comes to the problem of suffering, and misunderstand the heart of some of the words of Scripture that are there to strengthen and sustain us—as we'll see.

WAKE UP, LITTLE GIRL

Ali doesn't remember how she ended up in his flat.

Week after week, from the age of just seven through to fifteen, he subjected her to the most hideous abuse: physical, emotional, sexual. Those years are a blur now to Ali, a jagged fog of desolate memories. "God has told me to do this," he would say, brandishing a Bible at her, bellowing words of Scripture and causing the Bible to become a source of untold terror to her.

An object of use to a man with a Bible.

His actions left her numb, trapped in a cage of stupor, paralysed by all that was done to her body, mind and spirit. She locked her brokenness away somewhere deep inside.

Years later, when a colleague invited her to a church concert, Ali's initial response was to flee. Anything to do with God and faith exposed the fear she'd buried so deeply, the cloudy memories of the man and his Bible, of being all used up in the name of this God. Yet a tiny, hidden-away part of her was attracted by the invitation.

That night Ali gave her life to Jesus, and over the next few years began to find freedom as a daughter of God. All these years the lost little girl inside had been sleeping, and now it was time for her to hear the words of Jesus whispering in her ear, so gently: "*Talitha koum!*" ("Little girl, I say to you, get up!", Mark 5 v 41).

Jesus wept with her in the room she'd locked away for so long, and she awoke to a new hope soaring through her soul and flowing through her bruised and broken body. And God turned her experience in the depths of darkness upside down: words of Scripture, once such a horror to her soul, became her delight, a place of rest and peace beyond understanding.

While God did a deep work of healing in Ali, she still lives with the raw edges of the ruins of her early life. One thing that disturbs these edges is the idea that there must be some kind of *redeeming purpose* (for which read *usefulness*) in what she went through—the idea that God deliberately made this happen to achieve a particular purpose through her pain. She struggles to speak freely about her past, and she has been made to feel guilty by those who have told her that she should be allowing God to use her to help other survivors of abuse—after all, that must be what God was planning all along.

The problem is that some want to find a specific useful-ness in Ali's pain—it must be a means to help others. Perhaps that helps them to feel better about the things that happened to her. But it doesn't make Ali feel better—and it misses the miracle of transformation in her life. God has tenderly drawn her into a place of intimacy with him, and in that process, she continues to become more like Jesus as she passionately pursues the things of God. In that sense, God *has* worked in and through Ali's suffering—but this is very different to saying that God ordained the trauma to extract usefulness from it. To be told that God wants to use her, and her past, is to take Ali back into a time she was actually *used*. Instead, she now experiences the beauty of God's saving work in her, giving thanks for a love that shattered the pain of being useful to somebody else.

Have you ever been led to feel as though your pain is just a tool to God? Perhaps others have praised the fruit of any difficult times you have experienced, but your battle-scars are left unacknowledged and untended in the light of the good they have brought about. Maybe, you think, you shouldn't mind them as much as you do. Or maybe you have questioned God's purposes in your struggles: if God really did plan them, where does that leave you in your relationship with God? How can God be your loving Father when he gave you more than you could bear in order to use you in your adversity?

These are the big questions, and we must address them to come to terms with what it means for God to work all things to the good. God does work in and through our pain—remember Tracy's words from the last chapter: "God turned my weakness to his glory". God even works through the everyday messes we find ourselves in—and we know that these things help us to grow. But how can we find a new language to express God's work in our weakness, while holding onto the profound truth of God's love and his abiding with us where we are?

WHAT DOESN'T KILL YOU...

...*makes you stronger.* It's a well-worn meme, an Instagram cliché, a line from a song about empowerment that doesn't always feel very empowering when we are in the pit. The idea that afflictions work transformation in us is actually rooted in Scripture, but we need to be careful about how we understand and apply that Scripture. In the Bible's words are deep pools of hope that can console us and invigorate us all at the same time, where we find that even when we are weak and weary, God is working; even when the tribulations seem too much, we stand in God's grace and assurance. But this is very different to saying that we can find *usefulness* in adversity.

God brings about his good purposes through all our experiences (Romans 8 v 28), and God's strength is made perfect in weakness (2 Corinthians 12 v 7-10). I know that God has worked through my own experience of lifelong illness to help others, and that is a joy to me. Yet there is a gaping distance between the language of love and the language of use. In one, our pain leads to hope, assurance and authentic change; in the other, our pain is a tool to deploy without thought of what it does to us.

As we've already noted, God gives us an upside-down lens on the difficulties we face as Christians living in a broken world. Paul's words in Romans 5 are particularly compelling—and challenging:

> *And we boast in the hope of the glory of God. Not only so, but we also glory in our sufferings, because we know that suffering produces perseverance; perseverance, character; and character, hope. And hope does not put*

us to shame, because God's love has been poured out
into our hearts through the Holy Spirit.

(Romans 5 v 2-5)

In the first few chapters of Romans, Paul has been laying a theological foundation in order that we understand and appreciate the vastness of salvation. He's examined sin, righteousness, and Jesus' saving work on the cross. Romans 5 takes us on a wild ride into hope, describing some of the incredible benefits of our being declared righteous through faith. We have peace, we have hope and we have love. And it is these that carry us through when hardships hit, so that we can do more than simply cope; we can glory in them.

Paul isn't writing a theoretical treatise, an idealised version of Christian behaviour; he writes from grim experience. He acknowledges this with lists of great hardships and appeals to God to take his pain away. But the heart of Paul's teaching is a change of perspective:

I consider that our present sufferings are not worth
comparing with the glory that will be revealed in us.

(Romans 8 v 18)

Ask yourself this question: does Paul mean that our suffering does not matter? Or is he pointing to something different—to a way of viewing our pain through the lens of future hope? Hope is a remarkable thing; it keeps us going through the most hideous of situations. Paul is drawing on this truth to help us reframe our suffering into something incomparable to what will one day be our reality—when mourning and pain flee away.

Paul doesn't say that we glory *because* of our suffering, but *in* our suffering (Romans 5 v 3). We do not have to give the glory to the suffering itself, but to God who is with us within the suffering. We exult because Christ is in there with us, drenching us in freedom. We don't have to see hardship as something imposed on us to make us useful people, but as something we grow in and through.

A CHAIN OF GROWTH

Now, I don't know about you, but I don't often feel like I rejoice in my difficulties and pain. And I certainly don't wish to think of my suffering bringing about good when I am knee-deep in it. I just want to get through it. But Paul's inside-out thinking gives us a chain of growth that develops through trials in our lives—and helps us to view them through the lens of hope even while still living within their grip. This chain of growth includes three steps:

1. Suffering leads to perseverance.
The first thing to note about this is that the word Paul uses for "suffering" is not a platitude. It's a word infused with strength and depth, covering a wide range of trials of body, mind and spirit. Paul isn't just talking about persecution in this passage; he's calling to mind all the suffering, all the anger, all the pain.

When we hold onto the assurance that we stand firm in Christ through difficult times, significant endurance is built in our faith. The more we forge this kind of persever-ance when life hurts, the more robust our faith becomes. But endurance alone is not enough...

2. Perseverance leads to character.

In the Greek, the emphasis for the word translated "character" here is *dokime*, which means "the process or result of proving". This is a tried, tested and approved kind of character. The endurance we develop when we lean on God and allow God to shape us within our struggles leads to a more authentic, proven faith and character.

When we think about God shaping our character, we tend to think of how God changes us—for example, making us more patient, kind, gentle or self-controlled. It's easy to assume that God's shaping of our character is essentially about making us "better people", yet that sounds callous and cold—as if God uses the blunt instrument of suffering to force character growth. But what God is really doing in shaping us is turning our hearts towards him. The fruits of the Spirit are worked into our character as we respond to God.

What is our suffering, then? Do you think that God is imposing trials upon us in order to force us to change, or that he is drawing us to him and making us more like Christ within the trials? These two ideas may sound similar, but they are very different.

3. Character leads to hope.

Paul's chain of growth does not end in struggle. It culminates with the big picture, the future reality, the not-yet so bursting with light that it spills into the present. This hope is too big to disappoint, too powerful to shame, because it is hope born in Jesus' saving work on the cross and his resurrection to glorious life. This hope is almost tangible, and it is so potent because of God's love, liberally "poured out" upon us (Romans 5 v 5). This is abundant language. God does not keep love from us, dealing it out in miserly drips or occasional words. God cascades boundless love into our hearts.

What, then, can we say about adversity? We can say that it shapes us, certainly. We can say that it builds perseverance in us. We can also say that it hurts, and that we must lament when we need to lament. And then we can say that, in the deep mystery of faith, adversity grows hope within us. Sometimes, hope seems ragged around the edges, impossible to collect together and lean upon—but those edges still call to us with enticing wonder, blazing through the darkness and drawing us into pain-tinted peace.

This is all very different to a narrative that names suffering as an instrument of use, and us as tools to be picked up and put down—twisted with pain and then left to deal with it. God's story places love at the centre of our pain, and so we have strength to go on. We persevere, our characters are built and proven, and we plunge into healing rivers of endless hope.

Yes, God does work through our difficulties—but when we make this the focus and reason for our pain, we lose out on the bigger picture of who we are in God. God is doing the lifelong and life-giving work of sanctification in us, bringing us closer to him and towards more Christ-like character. This transformation also leads us to embrace a bigger picture of who we can be to one another: weakness can draw us together, our renewed dependence on God translating to a fresh and authentic dependence on one another—so that we encourage one another to pursue Jesus more closely and find him there with us in the desolate places. This isn't about being *useful* to one another; it's something with far greater depth. It's a mutual expression of living hope.

This is so much more glorious than the idea of pain as usefulness.

A BETTER WEAKNESS LANGUAGE

What about you?

Do you think you have ever internalised a script of use rather than a poem full of love? Do you ever feel as though your suffering is justified because you are being used? In the end, this kind of thinking breaks down when faced with actual pain. Think about Job and his well-meaning friends. They try to justify his pain in all kinds of ways, telling him that he must have sinned (Job 4 v 7-8), or his children must have sinned (8 v 4); they're increasingly desperate to find a reason for his suffering. In the end, though, none of these words help and God is angry with these friends, telling them they have given Job bad counsel (42 v 7). As the book closes, Job has not found any easy answers, but he has both held true to and found hope in his Creator God—a God who draws him out to the fathomless borders of holy mystery rather than giving him justification for the use of his sorrow.

Perhaps we need to explore fresh ways to approach brokenness. Thinking of ourselves as being "useful in adversity" can minimise suffering and even remove person-hood—after all, we are more than our struggle. Maybe, instead, if we think of God at the centre of the brokenness, joining in with our pain and working in and through it to build up our hope, we can live a much more glorious story.

How can we build this new story? When Paul invites us to exult in our suffering (Romans 5 v 3) he is urging us to apply a new perspective when life is hard. It's a perspective that doesn't come easily, but one that shatters the chains of usefulness. It's an authentic, lament-tinged statement of faith, a holding to the hope we know is set before us and a decision to practise gratitude for that hope—even when we cannot feel it.

AN OCEAN OF TEARS

If God only wanted to make tools out of our sadness, he would keep no record of it. The suffering, once passed, would be forgotten, marked off against some kind of celestial tick list: *That one is done. That purpose is achieved. Next!*

But I am so grateful that our God does the very opposite, and so this is how I want to bring this chapter to a close.

> *You keep track of all my sorrows. You have collected*
> *all my tears in your bottle. You have recorded each one*
> *in your book. (Psalm 56 v 8, NLT)*

We do not have a God who discounts our struggles or dismisses them as necessary to a greater good. We do not have a God who allows our tears to fall unchecked, who tells us to pull our socks up because we are being useful. Instead, we have a God who guards great storehouses of our tears, each one known intimately, each one never forgotten, each one part of an ocean where love strokes the ripples and justice roars in the waves.

Instead of using our pain, God bathes in the ocean of it with us.

FOR PRAYER & REFLECTION

Father, when I stumble under the weight of my struggles,
Set me free to find you there with them—
Not outside, using them,
Or using me.
When I cannot understand your silence,
Sit with me there
And hold me.
Thank you that you work everything to the good,
That you are with me in the painful times,
That you speak to others through my difficulties.
Thank you that you collect up my tears,
You write them in your book,
You roar in the waves with me.
Amen.

- Have you ever felt as though you have to find usefulness within your struggles? How do you feel about this, in the light of what we have explored in this chapter?

- Read Ali's story again and pray that God will show you the depth of his love for you. What does this story tell you about the language of use and usefulness?

7. Into an Upside-down Identity

"Who is it that can tell me who I am?"
Shakespeare's King Lear asks this eternal question when he is bowed beneath the weight of the loss of his former greatness. It's the existential mystery we all want to know the answer to as we cry out for the belonging we crave. *Who am I, really, deep inside, underneath all the masks I wear? Who am I at the wildest edges of my soul? Who am I in the desperate yearnings I cry out when nobody else is listening?*

Those questions churn through our minds in the times we *should* feel least alone and most understood. Chatting with our church family at coffee time. Surrounded by a crowd of friends in the pub. When our social-media posts are well-liked, but underneath we still don't feel seen.

When we feel useless, the question of who we really are haunts us even more. We hang on to assurances that becoming useful—successful, whole, better at being a Christian—will close that great chasm of yearning. But these promises can lead us to places that wound us further.

We've just been exploring some new perspectives on weakness: as a place of encounter, where we are strengthened, where we come closer to God and where God turns our struggles to the good. We've seen how, first and foremost, we are recipients of God's love, and that this love comes through receiving, not through what we do.

Yet we *are* called to be active within our faith as a response to God's transforming call—and that is part of who we are. Earlier in the book we thought about how the stories of giants of faith such as Rahab and Mary didn't need to be confined to the idea of God using them; we also found that their response to God's work in them was both to receive and to give. In this chapter, we are going to explore our identity in Christ in the light of the same liberating balance of weakness and service, and see how God brings these together in a beautiful new way. If we've scrubbed out the word "useless" written over us, what are we going to replace it with? And what does it mean to serve God and others outside the bonds of the language of usefulness?

YOUR AUTHENTIC SELF

You've had a bad day. You messed up that project at work and your boss had a go at you, and then you got home and had an argument with your teenager/cat/washing machine. You're tired and fed up, so you slump on the sofa and scroll through Instagram, hoping it might inspire you and make you feel better.

It doesn't.

#livingmyauthenticself, goes the hashtag on the filtered squares of posed perfection. The families laugh together. Everyone is successful. Christians all seem to be serving in food banks and homeless shelters.

You watch the images flicker past and gulp down the wild

longing that pounds at your throat. *You're useless*, the screen shouts at you with great accusing derision. You're not doing any of these things, are you? What does *your* authentic self look like?

Here's who you are. You're a loved child of your heavenly Father, who has a different kind of vision for your authentic life. It's time to take hold of a new identity, one that shatters the borders of uselessness, usefulness, and God's use of you, and takes you to spacious places of transformation and value.

PIZZAS IN THE NIGHT
Bang!

I woke up shaking, my hands clammy with sweat. "Not again," I thought. I heard my dad shouting out of the window and buried myself under the covers.

I couldn't take this anymore.

Every night for weeks now we had been disturbed by phone calls and knocks at the front door in the early hours. "You ordered a taxi?" "Here's your pizza." "You called an ambulance?"

We were under siege on our Birmingham estate. The gang who gathered round our vicarage repeatedly tried to set fire to our garden fences and the church hall next door. They hurled a firework into the caravan on our drive, burning it to a shell. They threw bricks through our windows and threatened us with knives. Every night I struggled to sleep, my stomach churning with fear for what would come next.

If I'd had social media back then, I would have felt even more alienated from the happy hashtag posts. My sense of self was in the gutter, battered by sickness, bullying and a move away from all I knew, and this sequence of events launched an even heavier assault on my identity.

I knew this was the call of God on my life as well as my parents', but as the threats, the jeers and the broken sleep continued, I found myself slipping further into uselessness. I felt that I should be serving God more wholeheartedly, but all I could see was failure, my identity crushed under my own sense of frailty. This was our authentic Christian life, but I am not sure even Instagram filters would sanitise snaps of a burnt-out caravan or a front garden full of discarded needles. Nor would they give the impression that I was very #blessed at all.

Yet this was living in obedience to God's calling. And here's the thing…

I am so grateful.

Through those years, I discovered that life lived in surrender to God's purposes cultivates the kind of peace that can't be found in any other kind of identity. It's not always a peace that gives a feeling of warmth and safety. It's not a peace based on how happy we feel, or how much we achieve, or how good we feel about ourselves. Instead, it's more a sense of being in step with the Creator of the universe within the mess. As I witnessed amazing transformations in broken lives, I recognised that God sometimes calls us to difficult places to do difficult things, and that a passionate pursuit of Christ leads naturally to wanting to do the works of Christ. I now know that joining with Christ in these works should not be framed by our usefulness, but the holiness and fulfilment of heartfelt obedience.

God gives us an identity that keeps our souls at rest in a world that shouts at us to be restless. But it's also an identity that leads to wholehearted service from that place of weakness. It is our authentic self, but this is an authenticity that springs from recognising our brokenness— and seeking God within it—rather than always striving towards usefulness.

We've seen why the language of use isn't a healthy framework. Now we need to begin to tell our stories in more positive ways. How *does* the Bible express our relationship with God? Is it possible to affirm our identities as God's loved children while still expressing our desire to surrender to God without "God using" language?

I'd like to offer three ways of reframing this language: partnership, joining, and co-working.

PARTNERSHIP

"I thank my God every time I remember you," Paul says to the Philippians. "I always pray with joy because of your partnership in the gospel from the first day until now" (Philippians 1 v 3-5).

The notion of "partnership" is positive language that describes both God's work with us and our work with others within God's calling. Paul is talking about Christians partnering with one another here, of course, but he's applying it to a partnership in the gospel. We are partners together as we represent the work of Christ in the world, and we are partners with Christ as he responds to our prayers and works in our lives. (Matthew 11 v 29; John 14 v 12; 1 Corinthians 1 v 9; 1 Corinthians 3 v 9; and Hebrews 3 v 14 are further examples of the same idea.)

A partnership means that we take an active role, whether in a personal or professional relationship. It means bringing all our gifts and talents to the table, and all our brokenness and mistakes too. As we allow God, our partner, to lead us into transformation and holiness, we press in further to serve him and those around us.

Partnership with God is not restricted to the strong people, or to the people who seem to know the Bible inside out. Maybe you feel like you can't measure up because of your lack of knowledge; perhaps you feel like God would never partner with you when he has so many others to choose from. But that's a deception steeped in the productivity lie. If you want to take some reassurance from Scripture, look at Jesus' disciples. Why did Jesus choose poorly educated, working people for his inner circle? What does that say about kingdom priorities—and about the possibilities for you in partnership with this God who created you to be you? God partners with you when you're serving customers, or cooking for your children, or working in the care home. Partnership might look like digging for deep wells of compassion, or the Holy Spirit reminding you of God's infinite love so you can share it with those around you, or sparking your creativity as you explore the gifts God has given you.

Here are some of the synonyms of "partner" in thesaurus. com:

Ally, associate, companion, friend, accomplice, participant, helper, sidekick, teammate, co-worker.

Now go back to chapter 3, have a look at the synonyms for "use", and think about the difference between the statements "God uses you" and "God partners with you".

Which one would you prefer to have spoken over you? And how does this change the way you think about yourself?

JOINING AND REMAINING

Jesus painted a vivid word-picture of a vine and its branches to teach his disciples about the power of being joined to him and then remaining in him:

> *I am the vine; you are the branches. If you remain in me and I in you, you will bear much fruit; apart from me you can do nothing. (John 15 v 5)*

Rather than the idea of being used, which usually signifies a time-limited relationship where the power is all on one side, Jesus' picture speaks instead of abiding relationship, where when we remain in him, the true vine, we will bear fruit, and when we are apart from him we can do nothing at all. The act of remaining in the vine is a purposeful vision of living our lives in continual joining with Jesus and so being fruitful in all seasons. "Fruitful" starkly contrasts with "useful"—it conveys a much healthier, nourishing relationship. We are of the same material of the vine, moulded into it, with our fruitfulness springing from that absolute sense of belonging. And the wonderful thing is that the joining, and remaining, is a two-way process. We abide in God and God abides with us (v 4). There is no danger of being discarded while we are joined to the vine.

Being joined to the vine is not a stationary calling. It's a place of active growth, of looking to the needs of others, of the pursuit of holiness. It's a place where even when we cannot physically "do", we are still engaging in growth as we abide actively with God.

If, like me, you suffer with chronic illness, you may feel the idea of doing anything "actively" is beyond your reach. How can you be fruitful when you cannot even move from your bed or your sofa? When John Milton, the poet and author of *Paradise Lost*, found himself going blind late in his life, he wrote of a sense of uselessness. Yet in the same poem (his Sonnet 19) he turned to God, writing of how his soul was ready to serve his Maker, whatever his state of being, and reminding himself that God is served just as much by those "who only stand and wait" as by those who are able to be more active. (You can read more about Milton's blindness in Richard J. Foster and Emilie Griffin's book *Spiritual Classics*.)

We find more people who "waited" in Scripture and in history—Anna and Simeon, Julian of Norwich, Amy Carmichael. All of these had a deeply profound sense of being joined to the vine, giving us an example of what it means to sink our identity deeply into Christ, joining into a new fullness of life not based on circumstance or on works but on joyful yielding to God. They found that "waiting" was actually an active process of joining in with what God was doing—even when the waiting looked like inactivity to those around them. Some of the most courageous people I know are living in active waiting, restricted by their bodies or their minds, yet finding God working in and through them in the most unexpected ways. If you are living in waiting, be assured that you are as much a part of the vine as everyone else, and look out for those fingerprints God paints across your life, reaching out to the lives of others.

(If you are struggling with this, Tanya Marlow's *Those Who Wait* is a great read.)

Let's think, then, about some synonyms for "join":

Accompany, marry, tie, adhere, attach, blend, cement, clasp, combine, connect, interlace, knit, weave.

Reflect on those words for a moment, thinking about how they might describe your relationship with God and the work God does in and through you. Think about a God who accompanies you, who clasps you tight, who connects with you, who weaves in with you. This is a God who joins with you and a God who remains with you. Think about your life at home, at work, at church; then think about how God isn't *using* you in those places, but joining with you—and inviting you to join with him.

CO-WORKERS

In Paul's letters, the phrase "co-workers" (or "fellow workers") describes a meaningful and fruitful two-way relationship with God: "As God's fellow workers we urge you not to receive God's grace in vain" (2 Corinthians 6 v 1). In this framework we work alongside God, willing to do all God asks, with God working with us and in us at the same time. Paul reminds us to keep on working out our salvation, "For it is God who works in you to will and to act in order to fulfil his good purpose" (Philippians 2 v 13). Again, it's an active word, one that reminds us of God's call upon our lives—not because salvation comes with conditions, but because our hearts are changed. We are full of gratitude, compelled towards humility and holiness.

What could co-working with God mean for someone who is deep in depression and anxiety? It doesn't mean that we should pull ourselves up and just keep going, as though we're in the workplace and the boss is telling us to get on with it. One aspect of the upside-down kingdom is that God works in us where we are. God hears the unspoken cries of our hearts and works in us at our breaking points. In dark times, co-working with God might simply be choosing to remember God's work in us. Psalm 42 is a profound poem of lament for times like these, when our souls might be "downcast and disturbed", yet we still put our hope in God (v 11).

This notion of being a co-worker with God sums up the essence of all the language we have examined here: partnership, joining and co-working. All these words give us a new framework for growth within God's upside-down kingdom, where instead of being used we are joined with, partnered with, worked with, remained with.

And loved.

#YOURAUTHENTICLIFE
#YOURCRUCIFIEDLIFE

Let's go back to the beginning of this chapter, and the beginning of all our longings.

Who am I, really?

All this language keeps pointing back to one thing: our identity is in Christ, and that means we find it most fully expressed when we centre Christ in our lives. Paul illustrates it with the stark language of crucifixion:

> *I have been crucified with Christ and I no longer live, but Christ lives in me. (Galatians 2 v 20)*

Putting Christ at first place in our lives leads to serving him, in times of struggle and in times of ease. The question is, what is the actual difference between us being useful to Christ and us serving Christ out of a place of self-denial?

My friends are adoptive parents. They have brought their children into the family and instilled in them a sense of belonging and unconditional acceptance. The children do not gain their place in the family through doing their chores or being useful to their parents, but through their blossoming identity as members of that family. Because of the love their parents lavish on them, the children want to bring joy to their parents' hearts (though not all the time—just like any of us, they're imperfect!). In the same way, our service to God comes from a place of absolute belonging. It's a place we've gained already, not a place we have to try to get by doing stuff.

The difference between usefulness and dying to self is where we are standing (or sitting, if you're like me). In one place, we are trying to follow a path with lots of signs along the way, telling us we need to go this way and that, try this thing and that, do more, do better, be greater, and then we'll reach our destination. In the other, we're following a narrower path, but it's not as confusing because we already know where we are going. We know the path because we belong to it, and we know that the views at the end are going to be more magnificent than anything we've ever seen.

Usefulness is trying to earn God's love. Dying to self is living fully and freely within the widths, lengths, heights and depths of God's love—a love which is already given, already known.

We naturally want to put ourselves first, and the world shouts from every corner that we should. It might be easy to think about building identity in Christ if life were plain-sailing and didn't seem to require much of us; but we all run into walls sooner or later, and we all have to make decisions about who we will serve.

So here's the thing:

Who are you in your weakness?

Who are you when you mess up at work, and your boss shouts at you?

Who are you when you're sick again, and the useless word looms large?

Who are you when God calls you out of your comfort zone to go and serve the poor?

Who are you when God disturbs you when you're watching something that's damaging your soul?

Who are you when you're deep in grief and God seems distant?

Who are you?

You belong to God. You are partnered with the Spirit. You are joined to the vine. You are a co-worker with Christ. You are a child of God's great Upside Down.

And now it's up to you to live fully in these truths, to pursue a truly authentic life where dying to self brings soul-freedom. This freedom doesn't look like a constant state of joy or peace, because it's a freedom born in the difficult road of putting yourself second to God and to others. But it's the most glorious, fulfilling identity you can ever live within.

It is who you are created to be.

BETTER BY FAR

Ultimately, our identity is built upon the certainty of our eternal future: living out our citizenship in glorious reality, where all the chains that shackle us are shattered to pieces, where to die is gain, and where being with Christ will be better by far (Philippians 1 v 21-23).

Your future is better by far. It's better by far than anything here, than any lesser identity you are living within, than any script that forces you into uselessness or usefulness. It's better by far than the best place you've ever been, than the mountain-top experiences of life, than your favourite ever day. It's better by far than anything your imagination can conjure up, than the sunrise on a clear May morning, than the stars displayed in glory on a clear winter's night. It's better by far than the biggest human love you know, than the greatest joy you've ever felt, than the wildest adventure you've ever been on.

This is not a human truth, vulnerable to change, tossed and turned like the waves of the sea. It's not "your truth". It's God's huge, magnificent truth. It's mighty to save and staggering in power. It's an upside-down truth, upending you until you tumble over and over into who you are supposed to be, where you remember who you are by remembering whose you are.

Are you ready to take hold of your identity in a better-by-far story? Are you ready to fling away your authentic life and live your crucified life?

Are you ready to be liberated into utmost you?

FOR PRAYER & REFLECTION

Father, when the images of the world haunt my dreams
And tell me I am not enough,
Will you smash down the lies?
When I am lost in boxes of comparison
And trapped by false identity,
Whisper your words of life to me.
Remind me I am loved, called, chosen,
Joined with and remained with,
A co-worker with you in your inside-out kingdom
Where power is reversed and love comes first.
Assure me of my sure and certain future,
Better by far.
Amen.

• Search through the Bible for ways in which God sees you, asking the Holy Spirit to show you who you really are. Here are a few to get you started:

> *A citizen of heaven (Philippians 3 v 20)*
> *An adopted child (Romans 8 v 15)*
> *An heir to the promises of God (Galatians 3 v 29)*
> *God's workmanship (Ephesians 2 v 10)*
> *A new creation (2 Corinthians 5 v 17)*
> *God's co-worker (2 Corinthians 6 v 1)*

• Reflect on the different words we've explored to frame the way God works in and through us. Do any of these resonate with you? How could you put them into practice in your life—and touch the lives of others with them?

8. Liberated into Utmost You

HE END.

I don't know about you, but when I get to the end of a story, I want things all tied up, all the loose ends resolved. When I taught young children, I loved the way they waited for the happy ending at story time, their eyes wide open, their breath drawn in. They longed for those conclusive, consoling words: *And they all lived happily ever after.*

But the end of this story doesn't throw up a nice, neat gathering-in of all the threads of our lives. Being unchained from the narrative of uselessness and usefulness is glorious and liberating, but it doesn't mean everything is going to be perfect. Because real life is more complicated than fiction. Life throws up illnesses, failures, losses, depression. Life makes us weak.

But useless? Used? No.

We've been finding ourselves in a new story of living hope, which draws us into freedom within our struggles. This hope gives us assurance that one day we will be most fully ourselves, we will be who we were created to be, we will be who we are at our very utmost.

We've been exploring our identity, and the new language of our relationship with God—a language that allows for weakness. We've been thinking about a new type of relationship with God, one that calls us to partnership, joining, and working together with him. But there's one more thing to say, and this will help us to stop falling back into old patterns of thinking. As well as thinking about what our identity in Christ is like, we will find our utmost joy and fulfilment in considering what it is *for*. What *we* are for.

So here's the question as we take our final steps through this journey: are we ready to live in the Upside Down?

To actually live within it:

immersed,
submerged,
engrossed,
mesmerised,
consumed?

This is the end of this book. But it's only the beginning of a new story for us all—a story that will take us beyond the bonds of the oppression of use and carry us to spacious places where the productivity lie is strangled by thorns and the freedom of perfect love grows radiant and magnificent.

A TORN-CURTAIN HOPE

She is crushed.

Wrenched apart as though she has been torn limb from limb, all her edges jagged and bare as she sits at the foot of the cross. He has uttered his last words and now he is dead. *This wasn't supposed to happen*, she thinks, the words a long low howl of grief bouncing off the corners of her mind. He is her son. She has seen him do such incredible things. He wasn't supposed to die, and everything is broken now. All her dreams, all her hopes, everything she held tightly to from the moment she held that miracle bundle in her arms on the night when the stars danced, the angels sang and her pain was wild. Mary had been certain, back then, that Jesus would change everything. She watched him grow and loved him intensely. She followed him and walked the path with him to this place. And now she can't even look at him. She kneels there, her eyes on the ground where tears and mud mingle together in a mess of pain and grief.

She hears the voices as if from far away, but really they are near her. *Leave me alone*, she wants to shout, to scream at them. Stop your inane chatter, your gossip. How can you be talking about... what? A *curtain*? When the sky is cloaked in darkness and I am soaked in agony?

A curtain? Her mind picks over the word. Tunes in to what they are actually saying, those people standing around the edges, their faces stamped with confusion and something like wonder. It's the curtain in the temple, she realises. They are saying something about a rip... from top to bottom? It happened just as Jesus died, they are saying. That can't be right, can it? That temple curtain is made from heavy woven fabric. Impossible!

But something in Mary is waking up to something new. Something like hope. A taste on her tongue, a spark in her soul. She is torn apart, just like the curtain—but there is a space beyond, and it calls her in. As the ground rumbles below her knees, she wonders:

What if?

The cross is the central story in everything we've explored so far, and it's the central story in all our stories. It's a moment that echoes through history, a moment that defines who we are in Christ. And at this moment the curtain in the temple tore—inviting us to view our lives in a fresh way.

Come with me into that defining moment for a while, as we imagine how Mary may have felt, overhearing the rumours of the temple curtain being rent in two (Matthew 27 v 51). She knew what was beyond the curtain, of course. She knew that only the high priest was allowed into that space, the Holy of Holies, and only once per year. And she knew that she, as a woman, wasn't even permitted in the courts outside it. The curtain was a reminder of the barrier between God and humanity, between righteousness and sin, holiness and messiness.

And then, there, in that one grief-charged moment, that curtain was torn, from top to bottom. The holy place was exposed. The gates to the place where the presence of God was said to be contained were flung wide open.

I wonder if Mary's heart leapt. I wonder if she saw something in that moment, if the great wide-open hope of it spoke into her own pain. I wonder if she ran to the temple to see with her own eyes; if she realised that this was not, after all, the end.

Mary didn't yet have the sure and certain hope of Sunday to cling to—she didn't have our knowledge of Jesus' victory over death. Her experience of Good Friday and Holy Saturday was more darkness-drenched than ours could ever be. But I wonder if the torn curtain gave her something like a flicker of a hope she could not explain.

The writer to the Hebrews would later place this image of hope in a vivid picture of the certainty of God's promise.

*We have this hope as an anchor for the soul, firm
and secure. It enters the inner sanctuary behind the
curtain, where our forerunner, Jesus, has entered on
our behalf. (Hebrews 6 v 19-20)*

Then, a few chapters on, the writer reiterates the signifi-
cance of this fundamental moment: we now have "confidence to enter the Most Holy Place by the blood of Jesus,
by a new and living way opened for us through the curtain"
(Hebrews 10 v 19-20). Because of this, he tells us, we now
have "full assurance" (v 22).

These words are not just one more slogan to help us along
our way. They contain the explosive power of everything
that Jesus achieved on the cross. An anchor is a weighty
object, built to withstand storms and keep the boat from
drifting into rocks. In the same way, our hope is strong and
secure because it is built on an event in history, not just
words in a book. Our hope is built on a wooden cross and
a torn curtain.

This torn-curtain hope is a great assurance for us. In the
defining moment of Jesus' death, when his friends wept and
the earth trembled, the curtain in the temple was torn apart,
because his death rescued us from sin and brokenness, giving
us access to the presence of God. One day, we will know in
full what complete, unstoppered access to the presence of
God really looks like. Jesus' death and the torn curtain stand
as a guarantee for this hope; a hope which, born in destruc-
tion and pain, resounds through our pain, too.

This anchor of hope gives us our story of our relationship
with God. We are living in an in-between place—the weary
waiting of Holy Saturday all mixed up with the certainty

and triumph of Sunday. We experience God's presence, but not yet fully, as we will in eternity. This is a place of pain and weakness, but also of strength and certain hope, where we find out who we really are and who we are becoming. It's a hope that flourishes in the Upside Down power that raises to life and blazes out to all the world.

ENJOYING GOD FOR EVER

In this book we have seen how God's purpose in our lives isn't expressed through our work, or how we look, or even in our comfort and happiness. What then *is* our purpose? What are we created for, and how does that fit into the whole story of the cross and resurrection of Jesus?

Here is how the Westminster Shorter Catechism (created by an assembly of 17th-century theologians) sums it up:

> *Man's chief end is to glorify God, and to enjoy him*
> *for ever.*

I believe that these words are as salient and liberating today as they were 400 years ago. Here is where we find our purpose: not bound up with notions of uselessness, usefulness or use, not all tangled up with productivity and success, not oppressed by deceptive narratives that keep us lesser. This is our purpose: not to be of use, but to bring God glory by living in the reality of God's love, to surrender to Christ who sacrificed all his comforts and freedoms for us. This is our purpose: to live in the in-between space, where life can hurt but the hope of Easter entices us and calls us onwards; where we live amidst broken pieces but rejoice because the stone has been rolled away. This is our purpose: to put ourselves aside and others first, and to plunge into the joyful freedom of God's love.

When I gave birth to my children, I did not look at them and think about how useful they were going to be to me, or how they might support me in my old age. I was lost in wonder at them and wanted them to experience joy, freedom, and life in all its fullness. In a similar way, God does not look at us and think about our use to him. God sees us through eyes of perfect love, and wants us to experience joy, freedom, and fullness of life (John 10 v 10).

Our utmost, then, is not at all what we might expect it to be. It's so much more than we imagined, and it's not as comfortable as we might hope, and it's not as safe as we might expect.

Our utmost is where we allow God to join with us and work in us, whatever the cost—and where we enjoy God for ever.

UNVEILED INTO UTMOST YOU
The space beyond the curtain.

You crave it. You look into it and you see mesmerising reflections of more than you can imagine. You want to dance into it and become a part of it. You want to fling aside the veil and leave behind the old uselessness for ever.

One of the most powerful passages in Scripture comes in Paul's words to the Corinthians:

> *But whenever anyone turns to the Lord, the veil is taken away. Now the Lord is the Spirit, and where the Spirit of the Lord is, there is freedom. And we all, who with unveiled faces contemplate the Lord's glory,*

LIZ CARTER

> *are being transformed into his image with ever-*
> *increasing glory, which comes from the Lord, who is*
> *the Spirit. (2 Corinthians 3 v 16-18)*

Paul is referring to a time when God's holiness was too much for normal people to bear. When Moses came down from his encounter with God on Mount Sinai, he wore a veil over his face, so that the Israelites could not see the glory that still lingered there with his face still tangibly shining (Exodus 34 v 29-35). But that glory was a fading glory, because Moses couldn't carry it with him for very long; and it was a glory the people couldn't see, because their hearts were still covered with a veil, just as the Holy of Holies was covered with a curtain.

But when Jesus came, and died, and then rose to glorious life, there was no more need for veils, on our faces or our hearts—because he took all our sin, all our pain and all our mess, and he died with it heavy upon him, and then he said that it was finished (John 19 v 30). It was done. The most powerful words in history rang through the darkness of a grieving afternoon, wrenched apart a curtain of unbreakable strength, and then resounded through history as the faces of millions upon millions were unveiled. Now you and I stand on the edge of the holy place, unveiled and free, with access to God's holy presence, with faces upturned and hands held high. We can only see in part, of course, but one day we will see in full, face to face (1 Corinthians 13 v 12). For now, we can rejoice in the assurance of that certain hope, as we contemplate the Lord's glory.

But we don't just contemplate it. Like Moses, we reflect it—we mirror it out to the world. Biblical scholars are uncertain about the definite meaning of the Greek word *katoptrizo*, which is rendered as "contemplate" or "reflect" in various translations of 2 Corinthians 3 v 18. It could hold the meaning "seeing the glory of the Lord as though reflected in a mirror", as expressed in the NRSV translation; to "contemplate the Lord's glory", as in the NIV; or to "reflect the glory of the Lord", as translated by the NLT. In those days, mirrors were usually made from very highly polished brass or silver. When the sun was particularly strong, a person's face would become highly illuminated by this reflected light—reflecting its brilliance, just as when Moses looked upon God his face was lit up (Exodus 34 v 35). Moses was literally transfigured, "shooting out rays" (like a sunrise) in the Hebrew. He was captivated by God's presence, and transformed by his holiness.

In this passage, the concepts of both reflection and contemplation are contained in one big blaze of light: when we contemplate the Lord's glory, when we look into the Holy of Holies, unveiled and free, our faces are lit from within. When Moses' face shone like the rays of the sun, it was only a transient brightness, but we have this light without the limits of time or space; we don't have to go to a special place to contemplate it and reflect it out. Unlike Moses, we don't have to carry this light with fear of it fading (v 34). We are confident of our place with God, beyond the veil. When we reflect the Lord's glory, we take it to others around us and we invite them into the same freedom, where hope reigns and love pours out in abundant and outrageous generosity.

SHINY HAPPY PEOPLE?

Does this mean we should go around with ever-glowing faces, contagious for the glory of God, happy in all circumstances? Think about Christians you know whom you would describe as contagious for faith. Is their shimmer all a mask, or an authentic part of who they are? Are they always smiling, or is it a different quality you can see in them? I know a beautiful woman in her eighties who is radiant with her love for Jesus. She expresses it in her great big smiles, but also in the way she puts others first. She's always rushing from here to there, doing shopping for her elderly neighbours (she doesn't really think she herself is elderly at all) and talking about her love for God at every opportunity. This is not a mask. It is not a fake lustre, applied to show how good at all this she is. She hasn't lived an easy life—she's experienced sickness and traumatic bereavements alongside all the general struggles of life. She is honest about these things. But her luminosity comes from a place where the veil has been ripped away. The light radiates from her face in great sunbursts of life and hope— even when she is weeping.

What about you? How have you seen this playing out in your own life and in the lives of others around you? You might not think you are very shiny. You might think you're a bit dull, a bit afraid, that your life doesn't allow for full-on sunshine. Bear in mind that Moses was afraid, too. He thought of himself as a bit useless, "slow of speech and tongue" (Exodus 4 v 10). Yet he was the first to glow with God's light in a tangible way—in a way that a veil could barely contain.

You are unveiled. You don't need to hide it, as he did, because God's glory is free and accessible. You are shiny even when you don't feel it. You shine out with that ever-in-creasing glory through the work of the Holy Spirit in you, assuring you of your freedom in Christ and bringing you closer to his likeness. It's not a sudden step into dazzling light, but a lifelong process of intentional, true and proper worship (Romans 12 v 1). All you have to do is keep contemplating.

Your veil is gone, and now you can see into that space beyond, even while you still stand in your brokenness. Now you can access the golden depths of God's presence with no fear, drenched in holiness and overcome by love. It's there you find your utmost: not your utmost use but your utmost identity. Your old self is forgotten in the light of blazing glory after blazing glory after blazing glory. You are a mirror of God's glory, not an object of God's use.

THE CURTAIN FALLS

Here we are, poised in the gap between the world and the space beyond, holding out our hands for more. Here we are with our faces unveiled, our uselessness smashed to pieces in the light of glory we can hardly comprehend, and our usefulness without a look-in when it comes to our place as loved and adopted children of our Creator God.

At the beginning of this book, you might have wondered if you would ever escape the story written upon you for so long, the story of uselessness and the language of being used. You might have thought it impossible to see beyond use and into value. But now, at the end, it is my hope and my prayer that you have come to a new place of freedom from your captivity; a place where you can begin to under-stand how God is always rebuilding your ruins. It is my hope that in joining with God's work, in partnering with God as he partners with you, in remaining in God as he remains in you, you can run free and unfettered, your spirit lightened and your soul launched into holiness.

When you feel trapped in your ancient ruins, caged within words of use that hold you captive and untruths that shadow your soul, find yourself emancipated within the sound of a great rip through the fabric of your life. It's not a rip that destroys you, but one that invites you into new places. It's a rip of revolution, a rend of restoration, a tear of transformation. It shreds the curtains that keep you captive, cleaves through the lies that have shaped you for too long, hacks away the thorny growth of uselessness and replaces it with words of salvation and honour and value. It's a great roar of a rip through the fabric of time and space that came at great cost for the one who loves you most, and so it draws you closer and closer until all your focus is on Jesus.

When you find yourself steeped in the productivity lie, bound by whispers of worthlessness that seek to keep you there, know that your true place is to stand high on restored walls and dressed in praise, as you take your eyes off your own story and find yourself in the greater story of who God is. Find yourself lit up from within, infinitely valuable, your face like a sunrise as you keep contemplating, keep reflecting, and keep hoping.

Find yourself tumbling into the Upside Down.

FOR PRAYER & REFLECTION

Lord, when I am longing for the happy-ever-after,
Remind me that you hold me in the waiting.
Lavish on me the hope of glory,
The abundance of holiness,
The story of who I really am:
Valuable.
As I watch with Mary at the foot of the cross,
May I hear the rip of the curtain falling away
And dance into the space beyond
Where I am free.
As I surrender my life to you,
Take me beyond use and into your Upside Down
Where I may glorify you and enjoy you for ever.
Amen.

- Reflect on how Mary experienced Good Friday, and what the tearing of the curtain might have meant to her. How does this speak to you?

- How do you feel about the possibilities of living life immersed in this upside-down story? What steps can you take to shake off the burdens placed on you by having to be useful to God and others? What could it look like in your life to glorify God and enjoy him for ever?

Reflection Guide

DAY 1: OUT OF USELESS

Read Ephesians 3 v 14-19

These verses remind us that all we are is contained in who God is. Paul has described our identity as fellow heirs of God's promise, and now he writes a prayer which we can also pray for ourselves.

- As you reflect on these verses, ask God to begin the work of revealing your identity in him by assuring you of your rootedness in the depths of a love that is wide, deep, high and long.

- Write down some phrases and words that catch your attention. What do they mean? Why do they speak to you in particular?

- You are being "filled to the measure of all the fullness of God". How does that change the way you view yourself?

Read Isaiah 53

Jesus' original Jewish audience would have had great trouble accepting that this prophecy was one that foretold the Messiah, because they could not conceive of a weak and powerless Messiah, much less one who was "pierced and crushed" for us. Yet these verses told of Jesus' priorities for an upside-down kingdom.

- As you reflect on these verses, ask God to speak to you, in your situation, through this vision of a gospel born in weakness.

- Notice first all the ways in which Jesus is rejected and mistreated. Do any of them chime with you? Then notice all the things that Jesus' suffering achieved (v 10-12). What is the impact on you of Jesus' humility and sacrificial love?

- What power structures are reversed in this chapter? How does that alter the way you think about usefulness, wealth, success and happiness today?

DAY 2: GOD IS NOT A USER

Read Luke 1 v 46-55

Mary's song sums up God's kingdom priorities right at the beginning of the gospel story.

- As you reflect on these verses, ask God to speak to your heart about his character, and to draw your soul into praise.

- As you read these words, what strikes you anew about

God's story over the world—and over you?

- What does Mary's story teach you about the language of use?

Read Ephesians 2 v 8-10

Paul once again emphasises a gospel of grace rather than works—a gift of God, in which we cannot boast.

- As you reflect on these verses, ask God to reveal the value you have as his handiwork.

- As you read verse 10, think about the idea that "God uses you". Do you think that this verse justifies that notion?

- What are the good works that God has prepared for us—and are these ways in which God "uses" us? How would you describe doing the works of God?

DAY 3: A CHURCH FOR BROKEN PEOPLE

Read Romans 12 v 3-21

Paul's picture of the body of Christ is a radical and subversive retelling of the usual picture of the body in Roman society. In this passage he expands on how that works out in practice.

- As you reflect on these verses, ask God to show you your infinite and equal worth within the body of Christ.

- How do you think verses 3-8 speak against the idea of uselessness—and even usefulness?

- Read verses 9-21. Think about your church—what phrases describe your church as it is already? What phrases describe your church as you would like it to be? Choose one or two commands you personally could start putting into practice to speak life where there is brokenness.

Read Galatians 3 v 26-29

This passage underpins God's view of a church where inclusion is key.

- As you reflect on these verses, ask God to fill you with a deep assurance of your belonging.

- What does being "clothed … with Christ" mean for our relationship with God (v 26-27)? What does it mean for our relationship with each other (v 28)?

- How does verse 28 speak into your story—what does it mean to you to be "all one" with other Christians? How does this passage challenge the culture of some churches today?

DAY 4: A NEW KIND OF WHOLENESS

Read John 20 v 24-29

Sometimes we read this passage as one that only addresses doubt—for which we empathise with the very human Thomas—and forget to wonder at the weakness of the cross played out.

- As you reflect on these verses, ask Jesus to reveal his wounds to you and soothe your doubt.

- How does Thomas' flawed understanding speak to you within your own doubt and fear?

- What does it mean to you that Jesus' wounds are visible after the victory of the resurrection? How does this speak into the notion of "wholeness"?

Read Luke 5 v 17-26

This is a passage about healing and wholeness, yet it also gives us a different perspective on what wholeness means…

- As you reflect on these verses, ask Jesus to speak into the deepest needs of your soul as well as those of your body.

- As you read, imagine yourself as part of the scene. What is each of the characters longing for? What do you long for when you think about wholeness?

- When the paralysed man was lowered through the roof, which aspect of his pain did Jesus address first? What does this say about Christ's kingdom priorities—and about what wholeness really means?

DAY 5: A NEW HOPE STORY

Read Psalm 42

This psalm teaches us to lament with honesty when times are difficult, giving us new perspectives on where to go with pain.

- As you reflect on the words of this song, ask God to remind you of his goodness and love, even in the midst of your suffering and struggles.

- Notice all the ways the psalmist expresses his sadness. Perhaps some of these expressions of pain are things you have felt yourself. Yet hope and praise are woven through this song. Pick out some words and phrases that you yourself could cry out in your own times of lament.

- Read verse 1 again. How could yearning for God help you when you are downcast? How can you put longing for God into practice?

Read Psalm 73 v 23-26

When we try to reduce our pain to a tool, it makes us see ourselves as objects of use rather than beloved children. This passage helps us think about God's strength in us through adversity.

- As you read these verses, ask God to fill you with strength—the kind of strength that upholds you at the very core of who you are.

- Reading slowly, reflect on the way each verse expresses the relationship between the psalmist and the Lord. How do these ideas speak to you? Reflect on what they mean for your own relationship with God.

- Verse 26 gives a striking picture of God's love and strength within our weakness. How do these words help you think of God as a loving Father rather than a user? How might this change the way you experience frailty or failure?

DAY 6: INTO AN UPSIDE-DOWN IDENTITY

Read 1 Peter 2 v 9-10

This passage is full of the language of abundant generosity about how God sees us: not as usable tools, but as chosen people and special possessions.

- As you reflect on these verses, ask God to assure you of your belonging in Christ by flooding you anew with his marvellous light.

- What does it mean to be a "royal priesthood" and a "holy nation"? How do these ideas help you re-frame your own identity story?

- God calls you out of darkness into his wonderful light. How does this shape who you are—and draw you further into who you are created to be?

Read Galatians 2 v 19-21

Our identity comes in putting the things of God above the things we want, and in knowing that the path to life is found when we "die to self".

- As you reflect on these verses, ask Jesus to draw you closer to a life completely surrendered to him.

- Verse 20 shows us that being "crucified with Christ" means that Christ now lives fully in us, with us now living by faith in him, rather than living to please ourselves. How can you put this into practice in your life—especially in tough times?

- Reflect on the words "I live by faith in the Son of God, who loved me and gave himself for me". How do these words uplift you, and how do they challenge you to find a new kind of identity?

DAY 7: LIBERATED INTO UTMOST YOU

Read Isaiah 61

This hope-filled passage speaks vividly of the upside-down nature of God—and these are the very words Jesus spoke over his own ministry, right at the start (see Luke 4 v 16-21).

- As you reflect on these verses, ask the Holy Spirit to liberate you into who you are at your utmost as you surrender to God and throw off the shackles of use.

- Which of the "instead of" words in this passage seem relevant to your own situation? (Ashes, mourning, disgrace?) What are the words holding you down that you need God's "insteads" to break into?

- Now look at the positive words that describe God's "insteads". Choose some words and phrases that resonate with you—how do they point to who you are really created to be, and how can you join in with God's rebuilding plan?

Read Psalm 37 v 3-6

This psalm speaks of how God loves us and wants us to find freedom, refuge and hope, as we put our trust in him and commit our way to him.

- As you reflect on these verses, ask God to draw you to a place of safe pasture, where all your deepest needs are met.

- What do you think "the desires of your heart" means in verse 4? Does God want to give you everything that you want, or does this hold a different meaning—a meaning that fulfils you in a much more profound way?

- What will it mean to you to commit your way to the Lord, and how will that bring you further into a knowledge of your full value?

A Blessing Prayer

For you who have been shackled by a sense of uselessness:

find assurance in the truth of who you are as a beloved child of God.

For you who have lived within the confines of the productivity lie:

be liberated by God's upside-down priorities, where the first are last and the last are first.

For you who live in a wilderness of weakness:

be comforted by the power of the Holy Spirit, and assured of your equal place in a kingdom full of frailty.

For you who have been used by others:

know that God is not a user and you are not his object.

For you who strive to be more useful:

be unchained from your works-based chains, and know your value in whose you are.

For you who have hidden behind a mask:
be freed to fling it away and live authentically.

For you who weep in chasms of lament:
find yourself with Jesus beside you, gathering up your tears.

For you who have been caged into failure by unholy
wholeness stories:
find yourself fully whole in God's freedom-story over you.

For you who live out on abandoned edges:
be cascaded with warmth as you find unfettered inclusion
in your upside-down value.

For you who yearn for a better story:
walk the path of surrender and find yourself in the wilds
of great adventure.

For you who have found yourself scattered among ancient
ruins:
find yourself standing high on restored walls, arms flung
wide in praise.

Amen.

Acknowledgements

This book has taken me on a journey through excitement, sadness, aching pain and inexpressible joy, and so many people have accompanied me—more than I have room to mention.

Thank you so much to the team at The Good Book Company for believing in this book, and especially to my amazing editor, Katy Morgan. Your encouragement and keen insight have been such a blessing to me, even when I had to cut out all that ambiguous purple prose.

Thank you to Ali, Tracy and Lynn, who shared their stories in this book. I know your stories will touch the lives of others. Thank you for your grace and courage.

Thank you to all my family and friends, especially to Tim, Tabby and Nathaniel—you are just the best. Thank you to my wonderful prayer square, Dawn, Caroline and Sharon; for always being there and being awesome. Thank you to my Home Group; you are fabulous. Thank you to my church family at All Saints Wellington; your love and support have spoken volumes about God's great love. Thank you to my writing buddies, to all at ACW and especially my "writing posse", Claire Musters, Abby Ball and Lucy Rycroft; you cheered me on all the way through, and I am so grateful. Thank you also to all those who took time to endorse this book.

And finally, to Jesus. It's all for you.

COMPANY

BIBLICAL | RELEVANT | ACCESSIBLE

At The Good Book Company, we are dedicated to helping Christians and local churches grow. We believe that God's growth process always starts with hearing clearly what he has said to us through his timeless word—the Bible.

Ever since we opened our doors in 1991, we have been striving to produce Bible-based resources that bring glory to God. We have grown to become an international provider of user-friendly resources to the Christian community, with believers of all backgrounds and denominations using our books, Bible studies, devotionals, evangelistic resources, and DVD-based courses.

We want to equip ordinary Christians to live for Christ day by day, and churches to grow in their knowledge of God, their love for one another, and the effectiveness of their outreach.

Call us for a discussion of your needs or visit one of our local websites for more information on the resources and services we provide.

Your friends at The Good Book Company

thegoodbook.com | thegoodbook.co.uk
thegoodbook.com.au | thegoodbook.co.nz
thegoodbook.co.in